ARCTIC SOVEREIGNTY INITIATIVES IN THE CANADIAN NORTH

A HISTORICAL REVIEW, 1700–1980

BY

DAVID MCROBERT

PREPARED FOR THE PRESIDENT'S ADVISORY
COMMITTEE ON NORTHERN STUDIES,
YORK UNIVERSITY, 1982

Cataloguing and Publication Data

McRobert, David Stanley, 1959 –

Arctic Sovereignty Initiatives in the Canadian North: A Historical Review, 1700-1980

ISBN: 1468193171

ISBN 13:   9781468193176

CONTENTS

ACKNOWLEDGEMENT OF FINANCIAL SUPPORT

The author gratefully acknowledges financial support from the President's Advisory Committee on Northern Studies, York University and the federal Department of Indian and Northern Affairs (renamed the Department of Aboriginal Affairs in June 2011). The views expressed in this report in 1982 were not those of federal Department of Indian and Northern Affairs or of the Government of Canada.

This report is dedicated to my mother, Dr. Laurie McRobert, who urged me to read the Montreal Star each night in the mid 1970s for the compelling accounts of its journalists who carefully reported on the vital work of the Berger Inquiry on the Mackenzie Valley Pipeline and inspired me to journey northwards to my spiritual home in northern Quebec, the Yukon and the Northwest Territories in the 1970s and early 1980s.

PREFACE

In the summer of 1982, I was fortunate to be provided with funding by the President's Advisory Committee on Northern Studies, York University and the federal Department of Indian and Northern Affairs to undertake a series of reports on development in the Arctic. I was able to secure the supervisory support of Professor Tom Symons, the founding President of Trent University thanks to references affirming my alleged academic competence provided to Professor Symons by my former professors at Trent.

This report is one of the three studies that I produced for York's President's Advisory Committee on Northern Studies that summer.

I have decided to republish these reports because many of the issues raised by the reports remain topical thirty years later. Indeed, former Prime Minister Paul Martin took major steps while still in office to remind Canadians of the "Third World" conditions facing hundreds of aboriginal communities in 2005 and 2006 when he began discussions that led to the progressive Kelowna Accord. In the 2008 federal election campaign, Prime Minister Stephen Harper "super-charged" the debate over Arctic sovereignty when he decided assertion of Canadian military, political and economic sovereignty would be one of his five priorities if the Conservatives were elected to office. After taking power as leader of a minority federal government, Harper began to implement this vision. Unfortunately, his incomplete vision fails to fully address the massive cultural, social, health, and environmental problems that a conventional, military-led and politically driven model, implemented from the economic centre in southern Canada (i.e. Calgary, Ottawa, and Toronto) is bound to cause for northerners, especially Aboriginal peoples, in the long term. As the Arctic ice pack has begun to rapidly melt, it has become clear that the Arctic Ocean will become a major trade route in the next 10 to 20 years. Pressures to develop northern mineral and oil and gas resources will explode, and precipitate massive social and cultural upheaval in the Northwest Territories, Nunavut, Yukon, Labrador and northern Quebec.

This report is part of a life-long quest that I initiated in my early teen years exploring the relationship between humans and biodiversity. The Canadian North served as an excellent introduction during the mid 1970s and early 1980s. To this end I am very grateful to Professors John Wadland, Tom Symons, Michael Berrill and other faculty members at Trent University, who encouraged me, in the late 1970s, to journey northward, thus reinforcing the messaging from my mother who had encouraged me to do in the early 1970s. I suspect it is a journey that all Canadians must inevitably retrace in spirit, if not in body, to understand the complexities of economic, political, social and cultural development in this country and the implications of this historical pattern for environmental policy-making and Canada's Aboriginal peoples.

Special thanks to Melina Laverty, a talented Toronto-based lawyer, for her helpful feedback, and suggestions for improving various elements of this report. All mistakes in this short book should be blamed on the author.

David McRobert, Peterborough, February 2012

INTRODUCTION

Each generation of Canadians has "discovered" the Arctic and, in a way, redefined itself in relation to it. Traditionally this re-discovery is accompanied by an expression of concern over our sovereignty claim to the islands and waters of the North. Various stimuli have been responsible for this recurring pattern, including: the exploratory expeditions of Franklin, Stefansson, Bernier and others; the transfer of jurisdiction over the Arctic Islands to Canada from Britain in 1880; challenges to our sovereignty over the Arctic islands from Norway, the United States, and Denmark in the 1920s; the construction of the Distant Early Warning in the 1950s; and, in our own generation, the voyage of the *S.S. Manhattan* in 1969. A wide range of writers and scholars has maintained an active discourse on questions related to these issues, developing an interdisciplinary field that is often called "Arctic sovereignty."

The sovereignty concept has acquired several layers of meaning, some of which will be explored in this book. Public discussion in Canada has largely, and legitimately, focused on policy questions that flow from sovereignty, from Canada's right to exercise authority over that of any other state over vast areas of Arctic lands and waters. Thus I will address the central questions raised in the past such as: what is the status of Arctic lands and waters? Which states have defined Ottawa's jurisdiction over the area in the past? How has Canada dealt with these challenges in the past? How well equipped is Canada to deal with such challenges in the future? What does circumpolarity imply for Canadian sovereignty?

These questions usually encompass matters of international law, diplomacy, technological developments, defense, and economics. In addition I would suggest that Canadian sovereignty in the Arctic cannot be understood in isolation from the concerns of aboriginal people and historical developments. Consequently this paper will examine all of the above areas in relation to Arctic sovereignty, which will provide a framework for understanding the significance of the North to the Canadian identity and the ramifications of this identity for future developments in the North.

Section One

THE EARLY PERIOD

DEFINING SOVEREIGNTY

The word "sovereignty" lacks precise definition in the literature of international law because generations of jurists and political scientists have failed to define it with exactitude. The term implies a relationship of superiority and subordination. Debates have ensured for two centuries to determine whether the relationship is absolute or relative in degree.[1]

State territory is definable as that area of the surface of the globe that is under the authority of the autonomous state and that is governed by its laws. The territory of a state is under the protection of the sovereignty power. Moreover, state territory may be designated as the territorial property of a state pertaining to public law in contra-distinction of private property. The territory of a state is not the possession of a government or of the citizenry of a state; the country is under the dominion of the *imperium* of a state. The significance of state territory is the truism that is the geographical area within which the state exercises dominant authority.[2]

THE NATURE OF SOVEREIGNTY

Before the Renaissance, feudal barons acquired sovereignty on the tenet that "might was right." The recognition of a claim by the pope implied that the authority of the whole Christendom stood behind it. However, with the expansion of maritime exploration in the mid-1400s, new rules were required and elicited to fit each new situation. For centuries, first discovery with the taking of possession by the symbolic planting of flags and the simple proclamation of the claim was sufficient to acquire *Terra nullius*.[3]

When the age of exploration merged into the age of colonization, discovery and possession were no longer enough, and the requirement of occupation became paramount. Consequently it is not surprising in the post-colonial era that international law recognizes a number of basic modes of acquiring territory. Oppenheim's classification, perhaps the best known, includes five: cession, occupation, accretion, subjugation, and prescription. In addition the supplementary doctrines of continuity, contiguity, the hinterland, and the watershed have been invoked in support of territorial claims and under certain circumstances may have weight.[4] Historically Russia justified its title to Alaska by asserting that there were "three bases" required by the general law of nations and immemorial usages among nations. According to Morris,[5] these were:

1. The title of first discovery,
2. The title of first occupation, and
3. The peaceful and uncontested possession for more than the first century.

In addition to these actions, the General Act of the Berlin Conference of 1884–1885 prescribed that, in order to make an overt expression of *animus possidendi,* a nation would be required to notify other nations of its claim. "The Berlin Conference was also responsible for laying the foundation for the modern requirements of international law, as later expressed in various international tribunals as '...exercise exclusive authority,' '...continued display of authority,' and '...occupation must be effective.'"[6]

Prior to the Clipperton Island case in 1933 (which is discussed in section four below), the above requirements were considered the basic political and legal obligations. It is remarkable that Canada maintained sovereignty over the Arctic during the early years immediately following the transfer of jurisdiction to Canada from Britain. However, Canada fulfilled these minimum criteria, with Great Britain's generous help, during this difficult early period.

EARLY EXPLORATIONS: A BRITISH HERITAGE

To a large extent, the claim Canada has made to the Arctic in the past century would not have been possible without the remarkable work of early British explorers in the Arctic. The fur trade was not very interested in land north of the tree line until the end of the nineteenth century. In fact, it was the search for the North West Passage to the Orient that led to the exploration of much of the Arctic coast of the continent and the islands of the North.

Martin Frobisher led the way in 1576 when he reached Baffin Island. Although he remained interested in exploring the North West Passage on subsequent voyages, his instructions were primarily oriented to mining.[7] However, Frobisher inspired others, and throughout the seventeenth and eighteenth centuries he was followed by many other adventurers seeking a passage to the west who found their way blocked by land or impenetrable ice. After the conclusion of the Napoleonic Wars, the Royal Navy took the quest up again. In the middle of the nineteenth century, activities reached a climax due to the many searches for the lost expedition headed by Sir John Franklin. As Caswell states, although the Franklin Expedition was lost, sponsors of these searches were responsible for much of the mapping of the north coast of the continent and the islands of the Arctic Archipelago.[8] In an ironic way, this tragedy may have been a blessing in disguise, in that it provided Canada with considerable information that might not have otherwise been collected until a later date. It is possible that neither British nor Canadian subjects would have explored these major areas until the turn of the century. This would have had many important implications for Canadian sovereignty in the Archipelago.

In addition to delimiting coastal boundaries, early explorations in the Canadian North inspired many Canadian legends, which shaped attitudes towards the frontier during this early period. To a large extent, these myths persist today in the popular impressions of the North that many southerners embrace. Demystification is in order if we are to understand the role of these men in opening up this vast frontier.

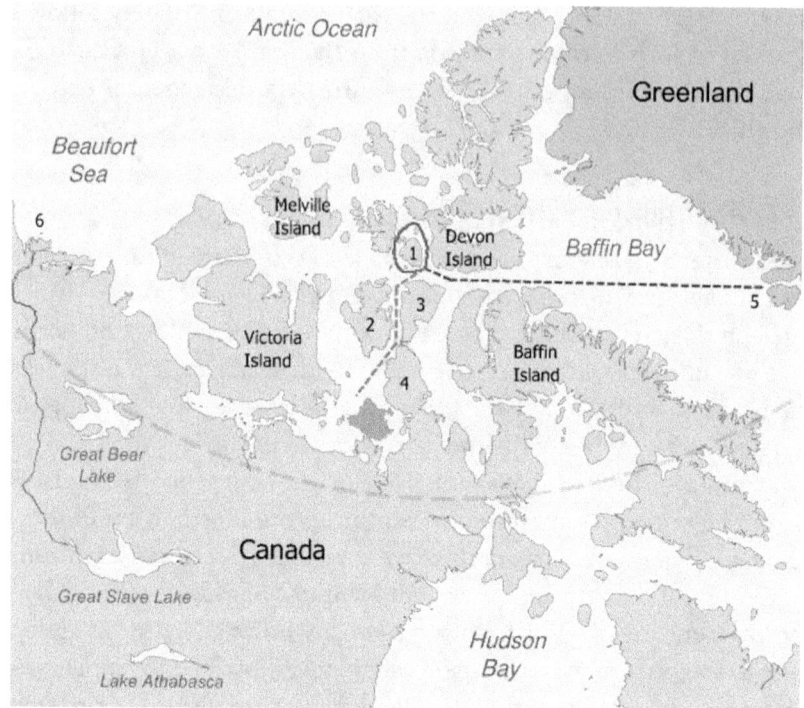

MAP 1 - Franklin's lost expedition - This is a map of the probable routes taken by Erebus and Terror during Franklin's lost expedition. Disko Bay (5) to Beechey Island, in 1845 Around Cornwallis Island (1), in 1845 Beechey Island down Peel Sound between Prince of Wales Island (2) and Somerset Island (3) and the Boothia Peninsula (4) to near King William Island in 1846 Disko Bay (5) is about 3,200 kilometres (2,000 mi) from the mouth of the MacKenzie River (6).

Source: Finetooth, Kennonv, U.S. Central Intelligence Agency, July 2008 as presented on the Wikipedia Commons, Feb. 2012.

For example, the tendency to mythologize Arctic explorers has probably also exaggerated the contributions of some individuals. Jones suggests that descriptions of Sir. William Parry as an outstanding naval officer, Arctic explorer, and scientific observer may, in fact, be unfounded.[9] Jones cities evidence that Parry was in reality a fairly ordinary individual who was without special scientific ability or leadership skill. Close scrutiny of records and naval documents shows Parry received his Arctic appointments due to his nepotism rather than his experience. His four Arctic expeditions had varying significance, mainly because he attempted to challenge the Arctic ice rather than fan out over the ice using sleds. This strategy eventually was seen as the main reason why many early explorers failed in the Arctic. Later explorers such as McClintock later found the sledding technique more appropriate.[10] Aggressive use of auxiliary steam power by Franklin was probably responsible for the failure of his expedition. I would suggest that the inappropriateness of this technological approach provides us with a model of how not to approach the North.

In addition to the formal contribution made in coastal exploration by the British Navy, it is important to note that much of the inland exploration was undertaken by middle- and upper-class men of British origin: John Hornby, R.H. Patterson, Gordon Matthews, Cosmo Melville, and Philip Godsell were British-born, while other traders, explorers, and adventurers such as the Douglas Brothers, who were Canadian-born, often had a strong allegiance to their mother country. Thus our debt to British explorers is quite extensive. It certainly established British sovereignty in the Arctic and prepared the way for the transfer of jurisdiction in 1880.

TRANSFER OF JURISDICTION

On July 31, 1880, the British Imperial Government issued an order-in-council transferring to Canada, as of September 1 of that year, all remaining territories in the vast Archipelago north of the mainland. The event passed almost unnoticed at the time, except in the inner circle of government officials in Ottawa and London who had initiated the transfer. In fact for a long period, it was unclear as to whether the Canadian government was aware of the responsibility it had undertaken.

The transfer itself was mainly a response to two apparently unrelated applications to the British government for concessions of land.[11] Up until 1880 other countries clearly believed that Great Britain could rightly assert a claim of sovereignty over those areas of the Hudson's Bay Company's territories that had been sold to Canada in 1870. In 1874 the British government received inquiries from A.W. Harvey (an unidentified British subject with an interest in undertaking whaling, fishing, and mining activities in parts of the Arctic), and Lieutenant W.A. Mintzer of the United States Navy Corps of Engineers. The uncertainty over how British officials should respond to these inquiries had potentially serious consequences, as the following excerpt from a memo on the subject from colonial office files indicates.

> *We must remember that if this Yankee adventurer is informed by the British FO that the place indicated is not a portion of H.M. dominions, he would no doubt think himself entitled to hoist the "Stars and Stripes," which might produce no end of complication.[12]*

In order to avoid the possible implications of Minzter's inquiry, British officials suggested that the territory should be annexed to Canada. When this idea was communicated to Ottawa through official channels, it was met with a favorable response. The proposed annexation was delayed by almost six years, however, as what seemed a relatively simple formality encountered numerous delays and some problems.

The factors responsible for the delay included "the unavoidable necessity for repeated communication and consultation between London and Ottawa, the pressure of other business in both capitals, and the lethargy over the matter, especially in Ottawa..."[13] In fact British officials are known to have sent at least two messages during the six-year period that advocated a rapid conclusion to the transfer process. However, other problems also appear responsible for the delay. Perhaps the more interesting ones were determining (1) the extent of Great Britain's entitlement to the Archipelago and (2) the mechanism to be used to implement the order. Concerning the latter problem, it was agreed that a "more efficient and less provocative way to accomplish the transfer"[14] would be to use an order-in-councils (rather than acts of British Parliament). It seems clear that the transfer was considered a high priority by the British government. Unfortunately the former problem was much harder to resolve, mainly because a satisfactory description of the delimitation of territories to be transferred was unavailable. As a result the document that was issued on July 31, 1880, had a meaningless description of the annexed islands:

> *After September 1, 1880, all British territories and possessions in North America not already included within the dominion of Canada and all islands adjacent to any of such territories or possessions shall (with the exception of the*

Colony of Newfoundland and its dependencies) become and be annexed to and form part of the said dominion of Canada; and become and be subject to the laws for the time being in force in the said dominion, in so far as such laws may be applicable thereto.[15]

As Gordon Smith points out, the new islands could easily have included the British Honduras, Bahamas, Bermuda, and the British West Indies, all of which were "British territories and possessions in North America" and were not already included within the dominion of Canada.[16]

In fact the ambiguous nature of the transfer did raise doubts in imperial circles about the validity of the 1880 transfer. These doubts probably figured in the decision to enact the *Colonial Boundaries Act* in 1795. This act retroactively removed the ambiguity of the 1880 order-in-council. It was worded as follows:

Where the boundaries of a colony have, either before or after the passing of this Act, been altered by Her Majesty to Queen by Order In Council or letter patent, the boundaries as so altered shall be, and be deemed to have been from the date of the alterations, the boundaries of colony.[17]

Further, a copy of the following explanatory note from the colonial minister, Joseph Chamberlin, accompanied it:

The law officers of the Crown, having recently reported that where an Imperial Act has expressly defined the boundaries of a colony, or has bestowed a Constitution on a colony within certain boundaries, territory cannot be annexed to that colony so as to be completely fused with it, as e.g., by being included in a province PR electoral division of it without statutory authority, it followed that certain annexations of territory to colonies falling within the above category, which had been effected by order-in-council and letters patent, accompanied by acts of the colonial legislatures, were of doubtful validity, and this act has been passed to validate these annexations, and to remove all doubts as to Her Majesty's powers in future cases.[18]

While this statement and the *Colonial Boundaries Act* appeared to clarify any confusion about the 1880 transfer raised by British Counsel (e.g., see the memo of H. Jenkyns in Appendix 1), it raised many questions about original transfer. Was this confirmation really necessary in light of the 1880 transfer? Smith has reviewed this and other related questions and he has concluded "that if there were any flaws in the constitutional aspects or the mechanics of the transfer of 1880, these flaws were overcome by the *Colonial Boundaries Act* of 1895."[19] The main reason the legislation was enacted was because the 1880 order-in-council questioned the purpose and significance of the BNA act of 1871, particularly in reference to the expansion of the provincial North. In fact it is probable that the act was conceived as a remedy for some of the serious legal and political deficiencies of the 1880 transfer that Jenkins raised.

These deficiencies might have translated into a serious problem for Canada had a challenge to sovereignty been mounted during this twenty-year period. Certainly a challenge was mounted in 1877–1878 when Captain H.W. Howgate of the U.S. army organized an expedition, led by a whaler, George Tyson, to establish a permanent scientific colony at Lady Franklin Bay, Ellesmere Island.[20] However, when expected assistance for the expedition did not materialize, Tyson became disillusioned and abandoned the project. Another American expedition led by Greely from 1881–1884 could also have posed a threat to Canada's rather tenuous hold on this region at this time. However, Greely had no instructions to make any claims as the expedition was essentially scientific and exploratory, a contribution of the United states to the First International Polar Year of 1882–1883. Indeed, as Smith states, if Greely "had orders to claim territory, it is certain that this duty-conscious and ramrod-straight military man would have defied the devil himself in order to carry them out."[21]

In reflection the transfer was clumsy and can be seen as a very weak consolidation of Canada's claim to the Arctic Archipelago. Fortunately for Canada very little other foreign activity took place in the Arctic during these years. Thus while Canada could hardly have been viewed as a sovereign power in the Archipelago, no other nation took it upon itself to challenge the tangled British-Canadian claim.

The six survivors of the U.S. Army's Greely Arctic expedition with their
U.S. Navy rescuers, at Upernavik, Greenland, 2-3 July 1884. Probably
photographed on board USS Thetis. Those present are (as numbered on the
original print): 1. Commander Winfield S. Schley, USN, commanding officer,
Greely Relief Expedition, and of USS Thetis; 2. Lieutenant William H. Emory,
Jr., commanding officer of USS Bear; 3. Commander George W. Coffin,
USN, commanding officer of Steamer Alert; 4. Lieutenant Emory H. Taunt,
USN, Thetis; 5. Lieutenant (Junior Grade) Samuel C. Lemly, USN, Thetis;
6. Lieutenant Freeman H. Crosby, USN, Bear; 7. Lieutenant (Junior Grade)
John C. Colwell, USN, Bear; 8. Lieutenant (Junior Grade) Nathaniel R. Usher,
USN, Bear; 9. Lieutenant (Junior Grade) Charles J. Badger, USN, Alert; 10.
Lieutenant (Junior Grade) Henry J. Hunt, USN, Alert; 11. Ensign Washington
I. Chambers, USN, Thetis; 12. Ensign Charles H. Harlow, USN, Thetis;13.
Ensign Lovell K. Reynolds, USN, Bear; 14. Ensign Charles S. McClain, USN,
Alert; 15. Ensign Albert A. Ackerman, USN, Alert; 16. Chief Engineer
George W. Melville, USN, Thetis; 17. Chief Engineer John Lowe, USN, Bear;
18. Passed Assistant Engineer William H. Nauman, USN, Alert; 19. Passed
Assistant Surgeon Edward H. Green, USN, Thetis; 20. Passed Assistant

Surgeon Howard E. Ames, USN, Bear; 21. Passed Assistant Surgeon Francis S. Nash, USN, Alert; 22. First Lieutenant Adolphus W. Greely, U.S. Army; 23. Private Julius Frederick, U.S. Army; 24. Sergeant David L. Brainard, U.S. Army; 25. Private Henry Bierderbick, U.S. Army; 26. Private Maurice Connell, U.S. Army; 27. Private Francis Long, U.S. Army; 28. Lieutenant Uriel Sebree, USN, Thetis;

See file:Greely relief expedition - unlabelled.jpg for a copy of this image without the numbers.

U.S. Naval Historical Center Photograph. Photo #: NH 2875-A; Author: Unknown Date 2-3 July 1884

Source: http://www.history.navy.mil/photos/images/h02000/h02875a.jpg *as presented on the Wikipedia Commons, Feb. 2012.*

THE BEGINNING OF CANADIAN ACTIVITY IN THE ARCTIC ARCHIPELAGO

In 1897 official Canadian activity in the Arctic began with the expedition of William Wakeham. Wakeham set out to investigate the navigability of the Hudson Strait at the request of the Department of Marine and Fisheries. A.P. Low followed him into the Arctic in 1903–1904, specifically to assert Canadian sovereignty over Hudson Bay and the Arctic Islands and to establish police and customs stations. After visiting a number of missions and whaling stations in Hudson Strait, Cumberland Sound, and Hudson Bay, Low moved to Cape Fullerton, where they established winter quarters. A police post was built there during that winter. The following spring, Low sailed northward to Baffin Bay and Smith Sound, where he landed to take possession of Cape Sabine, Cape Herschel, and Ellesmere Island.[22] Low also landed at Beechey Island and Port Leopold in Lancaster Sound. His report on the expedition was most valuable and included important observations on physical geography, geology, paleontology, ornithology, whaling, botany, navigation, and the Inuit.

Another central figure during this period was Captain J. Bernier. He made expeditions in 1906–1911 and was considered "the greatest island namer and claimer in the business."[23] In addition Bernier was responsible for the enunciation of the Sector Theory, a subject that will be discussed in Section Four. His efforts can be considered an important contribution to the assertion of Canadian sovereignty in the Archipelago.

As early as the 1920s, it become clear that its exploratory activities would have to be supplemented if Canada was to make a more substantial claim to the Eastern Arctic Islands. According to legal counsel, the islands had to be occupied. Further, the occupiers had to perform certain high administrative acts, such as establishing post offices. As a result the Advisory Technical Board on Northern Affairs of the Department of the Interior recommended that the Royal Canadian Mounted Police (RCMP) undertake certain symbolic acts. The presence of a police detachment was seen as a way to close up the front door of the Arctic Archipelago, but other forms of sovereignty had to be established to own the home. Eyre describes one of the humorous incidents that resulted from this bureaucratic imposition:

> *That symbolism was the key notion is best illustrated by a story involving Inspector Wilcox. He sent out a bundle of personal mail from Craig Harbour, with the request that somebody at RCMP headquarters either frank the envelopes or purchase the necessary postage.*
>
> *Postmaster Wilcox had no stamps.*[24]

In sum these activities may be considered a fairly meager program of activity in such a vast territory. However, they did fulfill at least two of the traditional requirements of sovereignty acquisition through occupation: "the animus or desire and intention to act as sovereignty and the corpus or actual exercise and demonstration of authority."[25]

EARLY CHALLENGES TO THE YOUNG DOMINION

Representative of at least three countries are known to have made challenges to Canada's sovereignty over parts of the Arctic Archipelago during the early part of this century. These countries were Norway, Denmark, and the United States, and what follows is a brief description of the course of events in each case.

(a) Norway

The challenge to Canada's sovereignty from Norway involved the so-called "Sverdrup Islands." This group of islands, consisting of the Axel Heiberg, the Elf Ringnes, and Amund Ringnes, was discovered between 1891 and 1902 by Otto Sverdrup, who attempted to get the

Norwegian government to support his claim, though he did not have much success.

One of the main reasons for this was that Canada was maintaining that all the islands in the region were Canadian territory, although the Department of the Interior generally acknowledged that Sverdrup had explored some hitherto unknown coasts of Ellesmere, Devon, Cornwall, Graham, and King Christian Islands. The Norwegian government's attempt to "reserve all its rights" over the island was probably a diplomatic gesture to ensure that Canada compensated Sverdrup himself for his efforts.[26] Evidence for Norway's apparent lack of serious interest in pressing a claim for the Sverdrup Islands is found in a Norwegian note of recognition dated August 8, 1930:

> ...The Norwegian government, who do not as far as they are concerned claim sovereignty over the Sverdrup Islands, formally recognize the sovereignty of His Britannic Majesty over these islands...[27]

As Smith points out, the "careful choice of words is significant."[28] In Smith's view the note does not renounce a previous claim but suggests that a formal claim was never really asserted.

In recognition of Canadian sovereignty over the Sverdrup Islands, Norway settled the status of the territory. Canada then felt free to compensate Sverdrup, very shortly before his death, with a lump sum of $67,000. In part this was paid out as a fee for his services, but Ottawa also aspired to secure any maps, records, diaries, etcetera Sverdrup had in his possession. However, as Zaslow points out, much of the documentation does not appear to have ended up in Canadian hands after all.[29] It is possible that the unofficial Norwegian attempt that was privately made just after World War II to revive the issue on the grounds that the 1930 settlement was incomplete was made because of the missing documents. However, the private attempt was even less persuasive than Sverdrup's and did not meet with success either.[30]

(b) Denmark

The question of Canada's sovereignty over the eastern part of Ellesmere Island in the 1920s was raised by Denmark after Canada wrote to

Denmark asking its explorers to stop killing so many of the muskoxen on Ellesmere Island. In their reply the Danish government aligned itself with a view of the island expressed by the Danish explorer Knud Rasmussen, who had concluded in an accompanying covering letter that it was a "no man's land."[31] Rasmussen, a noted ethnologist who had been studying the Thule Inuit since 1912, argued that their behavior was a reflection of temporary necessity and responded that he felt it was inappropriate of Canada to intervene in the management of Danish subjects. While the letter "added fuel to the fire,"[32] the setting up of a network of supply stores along the northern coast of Ellesmere aroused Ottawa even more. The supplies would be used by a forthcoming trans-Arctic sledging journey led by the Norwegian explorer Amundsen.

Official Canadian reaction bordered on alarm. When diplomatic protests from Ottawa went unanswered, the Department of the Interior took it upon themselves to organize an expedition that would sail to Ellesmere in 1921 in order to protect Canada's interests. The expedition was cancelled for that year but resurfaced in 1922 and became the annual Eastern Arctic Patrol.[32] Another interesting proposal would have employed British airships to transport Canadian troops to the site should a serious conflict develop, but it was probably considered too difficult to effectively implement without additional technological sophistication.

> *This airship was to be loaded with a group of Mounties and a winter's worth of supplies and launched from Scotland towards the Pole. Over Ellesmere the police were to parachute onto the island in time to greet the Danes. Given the state-of-the-art Arctic aerial navigation and parachuting technology, it is fortunate for the police that there never was a need to implement this harebrained pre-emptive scheme.*[33]

While the approach may be seen as "harebrained" now, it certainly did indicate the extent of Britain's and Canada's interest in maintaining the Canadian claim to Ellesmere Island. Further, many scholars suggests that it was Britain's firm diplomatic action on behalf of Canada that played a major role in quelling this potentially damaging challenge to Canadian sovereignty.

(c) The United States

Canadian authorities have always felt that the United States, rather than Norway or Denmark, posed the most serious challenge to the complete acknowledgement of Canadian sovereignty over the Arctic Islands. While the conflict with Denmark and Norway always involved defined areas that were within Canada's capacity to handle, the United States' stance challenged sovereignty over the entire region. The extent of their government's skepticism about the reality of Canadian occupation of the territory is evident in the following 1924 passage from Secretary of State Charles Evans Hughes:

> *It is the opinion of the Department that the discovery of lands unknown to civilization, even when coupled with a formal taking of possession, does not support a valid claim of sovereignty unless the discovery is followed by an actual settlement of the discovered country.*[34]

In addition to challenging the effectiveness of Canadian occupation, American officials and writers also consistently maintained that the sector principle was not particularly relevant and queried whether the vast areas that remained "unpeopled" in spite of Canada's modest efforts could be considered sovereign territory.

Uneasy feelings were further aroused in Ottawa when an expedition into the High Arctic by Macmillan and Byrd was proposed in 1925. Among the many objectives, the expedition's plans included:

1. To establish air bases on Ellesmere and Axel Heiberg Islands,
2. To fly north-eastward over yet unknown Arctic waters in the hope of discovering new islands,
3. To claim any new islands for the United States,
4. To fly over the North Pole, and
5. To carry out numerous scientific activities and test technological equipment.[35]

This slate of activity must have seemed a pretty tall order to the Canadian government. Undoubtedly concern was raised about the nature of the proposed bases, mainly because Canadian officials were worried that the explorers might well find some new islands east of the 141st meridian. As a result of this concern, Ottawa informed American officials that they would expect them to obtain permission for the activities they were planning to engage in on Canadian territory.

This action seems to have further clouded the issue. While both Ottawa and Washington were still negotiating as to the most desirable course of action, the expedition decided it had waited long enough. Although Macmillan and Byrd had neither explicit instructions from Washington nor the permission required by Ottawa, they made several flights over Ellesmere Island without establishing the planned bases.[36] Their aspirations were somewhat curtailed, however, when they encountered commander G.P. Mackenzie and the Eastern Arctic Patrol aboard the *C.G.S. Arctic* in Etah Harbor. Mackenzie held fast to the Canadian government's position concerning permits, and the expedition was abruptly ended.[37]

In retrospect this event probably reinforced the Canadian government's insistence that all future foreign expeditions observe conditions and regulations of operation and action in the Archipelago. While the United States government did not protest this procedure, it certainly did continue to refute Canadian sovereignty over the Archipelago. In fact it is generally acknowledged that the only serious doubt over sovereignty prior to World War II was the absence of formal recognition by the United States.

SOVEREIGNTY, ECONOMICS, AND RESOURCES

THE ROLE OF ECONOMICS IN THE ARCTIC SOVEREIGNTY

Economic factors and resources development have played major roles in the opening of the Canadian North. To a larger degree, the activities of miners, surveyors, whalers, and traders shaped the course of northern development during the early years. Their progress north demarcated inland rivers and established northern communities that were so vital in reinforcing Canada's claim to the North. This network later aided the government in establishing administrative programs, which were needed as a result of these northern activities. Their progress was not without casualties; both the environment and the aboriginal people inhabiting this vast territory were permanently scarred by their early activities.

While I am tempted to review the challenge to sovereignty from the oil and gas industry today, I have decided not to tackle this subject primarily because it required a fuller treatment than I can give here. Thus a historical review of some of the effects of the fur trade, mining, and whaling activities is presented below.

THE FUR TRADE

The fur trade in Canada is chiefly regarded as a dynamic but transitory force responsible for opening up Canada from sea to sea. In 1670 the Hudson's Bay Company obtained the first fur trading charter from London, England. After developing a flourishing trade in Upper and Lower Canada, its interest in Western Canada was challenged by the rival Northwest Company. Part of this rivalry included sending out men to explore unknown lands to seek out new sources of fur resources. Thus by 1793 Alexander Mackenzie for the Northwest Company had penetrated to the Pacific, and Peter Pond had earlier explored as far as Great Slave Lake in 1786 and established Fort Resolution. Pond's Expedition marked the first advance into the area of the Western Arctic that is not part of the Northwest Territories. Three years later Mackenzie made his historic voyage to the Arctic Ocean by way of the river that bears his name.

The period prior to 1821 in Western Canada was a time of fierce competition between several trading companies, especially the Northwest Company and the Hudson's Bay Company. Due to the intensity of the competition, the two decided to amalgamate, and their merger in 1821 under the Hudson's Bay Name "marked in a definitive way the beginning of control exercised by capital interests with headquarters in London."[38]

In the amalgamation of 1821, four departments were organized: the Montreal department, the Western department, the Southern department, and the Northern department, which included the area later known as the Yukon and the Northwest Territories. From 1821 to 1869, when the Bay finally sold Rupert's Land and the North Western Territory to the government of Canada, it operated one of the most successful monopolies in the history of Canadian economic development. Innis remarked that "seldom has there existed an instance in which monopoly control was exercised over a wide area through such a long period of history as in the Northern department from 1821 to 1869 ...The activities of the Hudson's Bay Company in the period of 1821 to 1869 deserve an important place in history of monopolies."[39]

A major problem that confronted the Hudson's Bay Company after 1869 was how to gather the existing fur resources more efficiently than their competition. Fur productions from the Northern department had grown in importance due to the depletion of resources in other areas of Canada because of settlement and the expansion of agriculture. Further, to a certain extent, stocks in Southern regions were also depleted due to over-trapping in the intense rivalry between the Northwest Company and the Hudson's Bay Company prior to 1821. For these reasons, the Hudson's Bay Company introduced steam powered boats along the waterways of the North and developed a network of stations into the Western Arctic interior shortly after 1869.[40]

Among the new competition to enter the region formerly monopolized by the Bay were John A. McDougall and R. Secord of Edmonton, whose furs, usually sold to the Lampson Company in London, and sponsored several traders along the Mackenzie between 1897 and 1908. There was also the company of Hislop and Nagle, which was organized in 1887, that traded at posts along the Mackenzie from Fort Resolution to Peel River and at Fort Liard and Fort Nelson until 1911, when they sold out the Northern Trading Company.[41] One of the largest organizations to challenge the power of the Bay from 1901 to 1935, when it finally withdrew from the North, was Paris-based Révillon Frères.[42]

Before the turn of the century, the fur trade in the North was a very distinct and different type of trade than that which prevailed after 1900. Whereas formerly the emphasis had been on trading with aboriginal peoples for furs such as beaver, marten, lynx, muskrat, and mink, a new trade involving mainly white fox furs developed with the Inuit farther to the north.[43] To some extent, this was a consequence of the death of the northern whaling era, which induced whalers to turn to fur trading with the Inuit as an alternate means of livelihood. While the interior trade was still active, its importance faded with the growth of the white fox fur industry around the Mackenzie Delta.

The Hudson's Bay Company (HBC) established its first post to deal with the Inuit in Eric Cove at Cape Wolstenholme in the Eastern Arctic (Quebec) in 1909. This was soon followed by another post near Aklavik in the Mackenzie River's ecologically-diverse and country food-rich basin in 1912. The abundance of animals that could be "harvested" (muskrat, fox, hare, etc.) in these areas helped the HBC develop its fur markets, assisted in part by the growing wealth of consumers in the United States. These US consumers had considerable purchasing power and a seemingly insatiable appetite for Canadian Arctic fur supplies, allowing the company to expand through the Western Arctic soon after its establishment of the Aklavik post.

By 1920 the Mackenzie Delta was experiencing unparalleled commercial prosperity. Both muskrat and white fox pelts increased in value; by 1920 the pelts were worth twenty times more than what they had been worth in 1900.[44] Other furs experienced similar gains. Muskrats were harvested by the hundred thousands in Delta, and mink was also a lucrative crop. Between 1919 and 1924 in Aklavik, the Inuit purchased, in addition to Western luxury items, expensive whaleboats and schooners to aid them in their trade. They had a fleet of thirty-nine schooners (nineteen with auxiliary power), twenty-eight whaleboats, and a few other vessels with a combined value of about $148,000.[45]

The price of furs continued to rise until the end of the decade. As market demand decayed, many traders began to pull out. In 1936 Révillon Frères sold out to the Bay, as did Captain Pederson two years later. By 1940 the Bay was supreme again. The fall from prosperity destroyed the economic base of many Inuit communities along the coast, especially those inhabiting Herschel and Ballie Islands. This resulted in a slow migration back into the Delta, one that continues to this day.[46] The main legacy of the fur trade in terms of Canadian sovereignty was the exploration of inland Canada, but the cost of this benefit was certainly very high to aboriginal peoples and the environment.

WHALING

Foreign companies began whaling in the Eastern Arctic in the early 1800s and finished in the Western Arctic by 1912. The effect on aboriginal people was not unlike that of the fur trade, although there were two major differences. The aboriginal people were of quite a different significance to the whaling industry. In contrast to their work in the fur trade, the aboriginal people were seldom involved in the harvesting or production. Whaling ships were independent resources collectors and processors. Additionally, upon the collapse of the whaling industry, the fur trade was able to take up the economic slack.

Initially British vessels harvested whales in the Eastern Arctic from Davis Strait and Baffin Bay, but they were soon followed by Scottish and American interests from sentries such as Dundee and Boston.[47] The prime target of these early expeditions was the manufacture of horsewhips and ladies' corsets. A vivid description of these mammals is found in Godsell:

These enormous creatures vary in length from fifty to almost a hundred feet, exceptional specimens weighing as high as two hundred tons. The enormous lips will yield more than a ton of pure oil. The tongue, with which he catches up the minute animal-culae upon which he feeds, is sometimes twenty feet in length; the heart weighs twelve hundred-weight, while the aorta is as large as a man's waist and through it, at each pulsation, spurts fifteen gallons of blood. A single whale will provide approximately two thousand pounds of baleen or whalebone. When "headbone" was in demand, and the price around five dollars a pound, the value of a whale in bone alone would run to the neighbourhood of ten thousand dollars. One whale, therefore, would almost cover the cost of outfitting and maintaining the average what {sic: expedition?} and everything else was "velvet."[48]

In the absence of any type of harvesting regulations, it is not surprising that shortly after 1880 the bowhead whale of the Eastern Arctic became almost extinct with this kind of economic incentive. As a result many whalers turned to activities involving beluga, walrus, polar bear, and seal hunting or trading with the aboriginal population for their main income.

The Scottish whalers, who employed steamers, established their base at Pond Inlet on Baffin Island. However, they rarely reminded throughout the winter or utilized Inuit in their crews. By comparison the Americans, who operated from southern Baffin Island, used sailing vessels exclusively and spent the winters in Hudson Bay. Americans frequently hired the Inuit as scouts during the summer whaling season and as hunters for fresh meat supplies or fur clothing throughout the winter. It was this contact that first introduced the aboriginal population of the Eastern Arctic to outside goods such as biscuits, coffee, molasses, tobacco, guns, ammunition, and Western style clothing.[49]

As the whaling industry declined in the Eastern Arctic, the industry moved west, and Americans discovered the rich whale resources of the Beaufort Sea in the Western Arctic. American whalers were drawn into the Beaufort Sea in 1854 due to the exhaustion of their own supply of whales in Alaskan waters. However, it was not until 1889 that most whalers became aware that the mouth of the Mackenzie River was open to maritime traffic for a longer period each season than the Beaufort Sea, and the industry shifted more completely. Pauline Cove on Herschel Island was selected as a wintering harbor, and two ships from San Francisco wintered there the next year. Following their success the number of wintering vessels at Herschel Island increased to four in 1892, seven in 1893, fifteen in 1894, and eleven in 1895, most of which made successful catches.[50]

At times there were as many as six hundred men who wintered at the mouth of the Mackenzie.[51] Throughout this period their impact was devastating on both the natural environment and the aboriginal people. The coasts were cleared of driftwood and the whalers introduced, among other things, outside goods, including firearms to the local inhabitants in order for the Inuit to secure food for crews throughout the winter. Without proper controls or regulations, again the whalers exhausted the bowhead, the beluga, and much of the caribou population.[52]

The social behavior of the whalers was very much worse than their assault on the environment. Abandoned crew members intimidated and terrorized many Loucheux. Liquor was dispensed freely among the aboriginal peoples, and they learned how to distil it. Often liquor was used as bait to lure local women. When single women were not plentiful, wives were enticed from their husbands and men were induced to rent out their wives. Reports of captains hiring Inuit women and capturing them from the Alaskan and Central Arctic coast were also common. Tales of drunkenness, murder, debauchery, and immortality swept back to Southern Canada.[53]

Public outcry and government concern soon became intense enough that the RCMP's superintendent of the district personally visited the Mackenzie Delta to investigate, as well as to collect duties on goods traded by the whalers in Canadian territory in 1902. A police detachment was established thereafter on Herschel Island, but it was doubtful whether they witnessed the whalers' worst behavior, since the captains largely refrained from taking the police to the whaling grounds and trading centers along the coast. Zaslow points out that there was a certain understanding between the police and crews. After this episode the few whalers that were left were relatively well behaved in the presence of the police, at least on Herschel.[54]

Some police officers such as Sergeant F.J. Fitzgerald ridiculed reports of rampant crime, while others, like Inspector D.M. Howard, made weak excuses: "of course their ways are not our ways."[55] In 1910 Inspector G.L.

Tennings concluded that the conduct of the whalers was no different than other nuclear family relationships in which the sailors took good care of their women and children to the point of enrolling them in schools in Alaska and the Pacific States. He did, however, suggest that proper marriages should replace illicit unions, if only for the sake of the children.[56]

These accounts were in sharp contradiction with those of Sergeant Fitzgerald's aide, Corporal Sutherland, who wrote:

> *A lot of liquor came ashore the first couple of days, but eventually it all fell into our hands. We took three prisoners, and if there was a J.P. here we could have pretty nearly tied up the whaling business. A Ruskie {Russian} fired a shot at the sergeant, but he was drunk and missed. I covered myself with glory by knocking the steward into the two o'clock next summer. He was intoxicated and refused to go aboard. We were nearly powerless except for our revolvers, which have been pulled out a good many times in the last few days. I thought I knew the depth of a white man's crimes before, but if you only knew a tenth of what these whalers have been up to! The missionary says that if we had not been here from the time the ships arrived, the beach would have been one howling mob of men, women, and even children.*[57]

In addition, diseases unintentionally introduced by whalers and traders eliminated a large percentage of the Inuit population. Among these diseases, syphilis was important because it caused widespread sterility. In 1902 a case of measles that originated among some aboriginals in Dawson City reached the Delta and killed about one-fifth of its Inuit population. The whalers imported Inuit from Alaska to replace the dwindling population; yet by 1930 the population of Western Arctic Eskimos (now known as the Inuvialiut) was reduced to about two hundred, of which only about a dozen could claim descent from two thousand inhabitants originally encountered in the region by Sir John Franklin.[58]

MINING

The Klondike Gold rush of 1898 spurred the first major mining development in the Territorial North. This discovery drew thousands of fortune-seekers to the Yukon who quickly exhausted the richest and most valuable gold deposits in the area. About $50 million worth of gold (in 1900 dollars) was extracted in a short period.[59] After 1900 larger capital-intensive dredging and hydraulic mining methods were used. Since the government did not provide much support in terms of capital facilities to these expensive operations, small and individual operators were soon eliminated. The gold mining industry lasted as the principal economic base of the Yukon until the 1920s, when base metals slowly began to supersede the decline of gold.

The first mine in the Northwest Territories was a pitchblende (uranium) open-pit mine opened in 1934 and owned by Eldorado Gold Mines Ltd. The mine, located at the eastern end of Great Bear Lake, was shut down shortly before WW II but secretly re-opened in 1942 to supply the United States with ingredients for the atomic bomb. The second major mining operation was the rise of a serious gold-quartz mine on Great Slave Lake in the 1930s. The three main mines, the Con, Negus, and Giant, were all closed temporarily during World War II, which disrupted markets, caused labor shortages, and aggravated the investment climate.

Following the war the federal government assumed a much more active role in northern resource development and expected that promotion of economic growth through non-renewable resource development would be both nationally and regionally beneficial. To this end incentives were created for the mining industry, including subsidies, tax exemptions, assistance programs, infrastructural support, and so forth.[60]

One of the most significant federal incentives was the "Roads to Resources" program, which started in the Yukon in 1957 and in the NWT the next year. Under this program the federal government proposed to finance the entire cost of specific development roads and to meet 85 percent of the maintenance costs while the remaining 15 percent was to be taken care of by the territorial government. This program, combined with John Diefenbaker's "Vision of the North" platform in the election of 1958, created a new perception of the North and was instrumental in shaping current northern development policies.[61]

A few small mines were developed in the 1950s, but not until the 1960s was there a great rush for mineral resources. Prior to 1964 fewer than six thousand claims were staked annually beyond 60 degrees. Between 1964 and 1969, fifty-one thousand claims were staked around the pine point area of Great Slave Lake and another thirty-nine thousand were staked in the Coppermine region.[62] In part this increase reflects improvements in exploration techniques, better transportation, the encouragement that some discoveries generated, and the rise of metal prices, but the role of government cannot be discounted.

EARLY ECONOMIC ACTIVITY AND SOVEREIGNTY

Activities of whalers, traders, and miners had very serious social impact on aboriginal people and were responsible for creating aboriginal economic dependence on Southern Canada. They also did much to color the nature of sovereignty in the Canadian Arctic. The disturbance of traditional lifestyles was so deeply rooted that it resulted in cultural and psychological problems for the Inuit and Métis, which continue today. To a great extent the administrative activities that were undertaken soon after the demise of the fur trade were the only reasonable response that Ottawa could have employed to solve some of the complex problems raised by resources development in the far North. Arguably reductions in the number of Inuit probably gave the impression to explorers that Canadian subjects living in the North were very few in number. Thus it made sense to integrate northern aboriginal peoples into the developing nation.

The most interesting pattern that resources development imposed on Canadian sovereignty was related to RCMP activities. Overall the growth of R.C.M.P involvement in the far North grew significantly during these years. More than any other activity, their presence established sovereignty in the Arctic.

Section Three

GOVERNMENT ACTIVITIES IN THE NORTH

ABORIGINAL AND INUIT ADMINISTRATION

Under the terms of the Constitution Act, 1867 (previously titled the *British North America Act* of 1867), the administration and welfare of the aboriginals and Inuit living in both the Yukon and the Northwest Territories (NWT) became a federal responsibility. However, it was not until thousands of gold-seekers flowed into the Klondike in the 1880s that the government felt it was necessary to begin formal administration of northern aboriginal peoples. In 1896 Inspector Charles Constantine of the North West Mounted Police (NWMP), who had been to the Yukon in 1894, was sent back again.

In his position, he was empowered to act for:

> ...*the superintendent General of Indian Affairs in Yukon country, to deal with the Indians in that country, and to take such actions as he can within the law, as may seem to be advisable in their interest; it being understood that no authority has been given him to make or negotiate any treaty with any of the Indians of that country, or to incur any expenditure or bind the Department of Indian Affairs or the government of Canada to any expenditure other than may be absolutely necessary for the relief of actual cases of destitution.*[63]

As many writers have since pointed out, this did not amount to much of a relief program. However, the church, which was now fairly well-established in the North, pressed for more aid. In the late 1890s and the early 1900s, the bishop of Mackenzie River, Reverend W.C. Bompas, requested help for Yukon aboriginals in the form of medical attention, relief, and education.[64] Under the supervision of the commissioner of the Yukon Territory, the NWMP were given the task of granting some relief and medical attention and selecting sites for aboriginal settlements and woodlots.

Apart from these activities, little in the way of social welfare assistance was granted to aboriginal people in northern communities during this period. However, on the advice of a federally-appointed commission set up by to make a treaty with aboriginal peoples living in the provisional district of Athabaska in 1899 and 1900, a new approach that would facilitate acculturation of aboriginal peoples was developed. James A. Macrae, who had been appointed commissioner of the district, held meetings with aboriginals from Fort Resolution to Fort St. John, B.C.[65] By the end of 1900, 3,323 Dogrib and Chipewyan aboriginals, primarily living in Yellowknife in the NWT and northern B.C., were receiving treaty money under Treaty Eight.

The next major advance in aboriginal administration occurred when the Fort Smith Indian Agency was opened in June 1911 for aboriginal peoples who adhered to Treaty Eight. Later that year an agency was opened at Fort Simpson for non-treaty aboriginals of the Mackenzie Basin. However, such agencies could do little to prevent the cycle of hunger and starvation that plagued many communities. The drop in fur prices further aggravated hardship, although it was short-lived. Fortunately mountain sheep and caribou were still plentiful, although not uniformly available. Nevertheless this did not prevent many young aboriginals from making their way to Edmonton and other more secure economic climates.[66]

In the summer of 1921, seven chiefs and twelve headmen of the region signed Treaty Number Eleven.[67] As a result aboriginal peoples under the treaty received money on a per capita basis for the 1,915 residents of the region who ceded title to three hundred and twenty-seven thousand square miles of land to the Crown. At the time provision was made in the treaty for the setting aside of reserve lands at such time as the aboriginal people indicated their need of them. As of 1981 this had not been formally completed, although such provisions from the basis of land claims are currently under negotiation between the federal government and many treaty aboriginals in the North. Between 1981 and 2011 remarkable progress was made on many northern treaties and agreements covering a wide range of areas such as environmental protection, education, social justice, and cultural protection.

Apart from the establishment of a piecemeal network of aboriginal agencies and the solidification of some communities in the North during the 1920s and 1930s, no other substantial activities in the field of administration occurred until World War II. The Second World War brought intense activity to many parts of the North, which employed anyone who wanted to work. In addition the CANOL project began that same year. Aboriginal peoples were employed in drilling at Norman Wells, the construction of an oil refinery at Whitehorse, and the building of a pipeline between the two centers. To a certain extent these projects brought a new awareness of northern social, economic, and health conditions and began a new period of aboriginal administration in the North.

IMPROVEMENTS IN HEALTH

Responsibility for medical and hospital care in the NWT and the Yukon was transferred to the Department of National Health in 1945. In addition the Department of Indian Affairs took over the former mission hospital at Fort Norman. This allowed the government to modernize the hospital and handle many cases that previously had been sent aside for treatment. The success of this conversion encouraged the federal government, and subsequent grants allowed other mission hospitals to also modernize facilities and obtain certified medical staff.[68] Further, a vigorous attack on tuberculosis, which was widespread, was initiated. Unfortunately treatment of tuberculosis involved long periods in southern hospitals, which resulted in heart-breaking experiences for the tightly knit Inuit families. In the end this separation was often justified by its medical success, however.[69]

Despite many improvements in the planning and delivery of health care in Arctic Canada, considerable problems exist in health care delivery even today. Infant mortality, infectious disease, alcoholism, and mental illness are all increasing. Future improvements are likely to be linked to improved communications and transportation networks, but Dear[70] has suggested that the main improvement must come in the areas of health education, garbage disposal, and sewage/water facilities.

EDUCATION

Missionaries provided much of the early education of aboriginal people in the Yukon and NWT. Roman Catholics of the oblate order and Anglicans first came into contact with aboriginal peoples in the 1850s and 1860s, although the first school was begun at Fort Resolution in 1894 when the Church of England applied for a $200 grant from the Department of Indian Affairs.[71] Missionaries also authored many ethnological reports and translated many aboriginal languages, although the latter task was usually undertaken from theological perspectives, with the production of scriptural translations foremost in mind. While the federal government often subsidized the missions, the federal government delayed acknowledgement of responsibility for education until the 1950s.[72]

Transfer of authority to the territorial governments resulted in more centralization of education programs. Schools were constructed in main settlements, although many of the children were forced to live in hostels in order to attend them. This was a fairly disruptive practice. However, the development of an advisory committee for education on a local level has since led to a decline in residential school enrolment because of the extension of grades taught in the smaller communities.[73]

Curricula have also been substantially revamped. Aboriginal teaching assistants are used to teach land living skills, aboriginal values, and new skills in telecommunications and heavy equipment operation. In the late '60s, many young aboriginal people began teaching Métis and aboriginals throughout the Mackenzie Basin. These factors appear to have stabilized the negative impacts of Western educational programs, which are described by Brody and Freeman.[74]

Other important developments have taken place in the field of adult education. Adult vocational schools exist in Tuktoyuktuk and Fort Smith. These courses will go a long way in accommodating the needs of both industry and aboriginal people in the future.

COMMUNITY DEVELOPMENT

The establishment of schools and nursing stations in main settlements induced many aboriginal peoples to move to these settlements from the small hunting camps, making it more difficult for them to hunt and trap. Because there were no significant sources of income for local residents apart from wage employment in service occupations in white establishments, relief became widespread. In smaller communities the improved health of northern aboriginal peoples served to emphasize deficiencies in a sedentary lifestyle. Periods of famine often followed periods of plenty. While new technologies such as the rifle made it possible to harvest many caribou at once, migration routes often shifted depending on climatic conditions and the changing grazing capacity of the tundra.

Economic and community development became a major concern for many aboriginal communities. In response aboriginal administration in the NWT was reorganized in 1949 with the creation of more regional offices and the recruitment of more trained personnel.[75] In addition numerous interim measures were introduced to prevent widespread suffering. Cold storage installations worked well in preserving fresh meat and fish, and by 1964 twelve more northern communities had built them. The federal government also became involved in the marketing of aboriginal handicrafts. Sales of jackets, gloves, mukluks, and moccasins were more actively prompted in southern markets, and federal action was taken to protect such articles from foreign counterfeit imports.[76]

Housing programs were also initiated at this time. In 1950 a settlement was established on Latham Island at Yellowknife and a number of houses was erected with government assistance. Another settlement near Whitehorse was provided with six houses, wells, and a pump house in 1955. In other communities small sawmills were set up, and aboriginal peoples were taught to make improvements to existing houses. Homemakers' clubs in Mayo and Teslin, which were established in 1960, provided aboriginal peoples with a fundamental knowledge of southern approaches to home maintenance and hygiene. Such initiatives further spurred the exodus off the land and restructured many communities, as Diamond Jenness so graphically showed. In fact the resultant cultural upheaval necessitated the development of local government, which has led the resurgences of many communities in the North during the past decade.

LOCAL GOVERNMENT AND THE CARROTHERS COMMISSION

Some of the main problems that emerged in the '50s were the result of centralized decision-making in Ottawa, as Hamelin argues.[77] The Carrothers Advisory Commission on Development of Government recommended that the NWT government be moved to Yellowknife in 1966. While this change was soon implemented, it did little to bring representative government to many areas, such as the Eastern Arctic. However, lavish funding allowed the continued expansion of services at main settlements and greatly improved housing there. As Brody points out, this led to further concentration of the Inuit population, making them more dependent on the government.[78] With little control over their own future and often unable to understand the changing administrative policies that regulated their day-to-day lives, many Inuit became demoralized, especially at the major centers where white influence was greatest and alcohol easily obtainable.

In many ways, Hamelin is correct in pointing out that a great deal of centralized power remains in the hands of the NWT government in Yellowknife. Fortunately this centralization has been offset by the evolution of local autonomous band councils, and more democratic forms of government were initiated in the early 1970s.

The development of local autonomous band councils has been an ongoing process since the late 1950s. In 1958 a new band council was chosen at Old Crow using a secret ballot for the first time.[79] Since then most bands have adopted democratic electoral systems and have become more actively involved in the management of their own communities. Further, the governmental structure for the NWT at the local level has changed considerably in the last fifteen years. From a few advisory councils and four municipalities in 1967, the structure changed to one which was comprised of thirty-three elected responsible councils and sixteen municipalities in 1937.[80] In fact only two communities in the NWT with populations over one hundred do not have local councils.[81] In part this achievement reflects the basic recommendations of the Carrothers Commission, which encourages the federal government to adopt a northern policy with a program for the development of local government. Arguably this program has been a mixed blessing for northern aboriginal peoples in the NWT. While the developments in Frobisher Bay and Yellowknife were severely disorienting for all aboriginals, local political development was responsible for the increasing political awareness of aboriginal Canadians. These grassroots activities have motivated aboriginals and the Inuit to become spokespeople for their own people on issues such as the environment, welfare, education, and land rights.

DEFENCE, TRANSPORTATION, AND COMMUNICATIONS

Probably the most significance legacy of the Second World War was the recognition of the strategic significance of the Distant Early Warning (D.E.W.) line. As Sutherland points out, the development of long-range aircraft suggested that North America could be attacked from the North.[82] This threat was compounded by the invention of nuclear weapons. The official response from Ottawa and Washington was to learn as much as it could about the North in order to provide a defense against this potential threat and develop counter-threats. In addition the following strategy was undertaken:

> In the years immediately following the war, a number of weather stations were established jointly by the United States and Canada in the Queen Elizabeth Islands to meet both military and civil needs, a chain of low frequency Loran stations was built to assist navigation, an oil pipeline was constructed from Haines across northern British Columbia and the Yukon Territory to Fairbanks, and air photography and mapping were accelerated. These steps were followed by the Pinetree, Mid-Canada, and Distant Early Warning radar lines, Strategic Air Command air refueling bases in Northern Alberta, Churchill and Frobisher, and sophisticated communications required for the Ballistic Missile Early Warning Systems. [83]

The effect of these very major projects on northern development was shown most clearly in communications and transportation. Communications systems such as the Northwest Territories and the Yukon Radio System, developed by the military, were turned over to the civilian authorities when they became outdated.[84] The Northwest

Highway system followed a similar evolution from military to civil operation. The same sequence occurred in the airfield system, which connected the northwest staging route. The post-war airfields, communications, and accommodation facilities are now mainly in civilian hands. Most recently considerable military investment has been parlayed into satellite communications and reconnaissance in the North. Presumably satellite use will follow the trend of military initiatives, which have proved invaluable to civilians in the North.

THE ROYAL CANADIAN MOUNTED POLICE

For almost one hundred years, the Royal Canadian Mounted Police (previously referred to as the Northwest Mounted Police, or NWMP) have been a powerful influence on the course of northern development. While many agencies now operate in most communities in the North, for many years only the RCMP formally represented the federal government, counsel for people with problems, and law enforcers. RCMP officers are also known to have performed many other functions, including immigration officers, coroners, census takers, recorders of birth and deaths, postmasters, game officers, and mail carriers. While Hudson's Bay Company personnel and church missionaries also performed these roles in the early years, it would not be unfair, in my opinion, to suggest that the RCMP did the bulk of this day-to-day bullwork.[85]

The main function of the RCMP was maintenance of law and order and symbolizing Canadian sovereignty over the North. This task had been ongoing in the Canadian northwest for more than twenty years. However, the RCMP were catapulted into the public spotlight during the Klondike gold rush in 1898. As Desmond Morton points out, a national institution in which "Canadians took extraordinary pride" emerged.[86] While much of the RCMP myth may have been based on romanticism and idealism, it is important to recognize that the adventure-seeking Mounties like Sam Steele did more than maintain order in Dawson City. Klondike was primarily an American gold rush. The RCMP symbolized Canadian sovereignty.

As mining activities in the Yukon began to wind down, the RCMP presence spread into the NWT. In 1903 a post was established at Fort Macpherson above the Arctic Circle and not far from the Yukon border.

Additional posts soon followed, and three isolated cabins formed the network necessary to establish the legacy patrols of the east central barrens.[87] Further, the RCMP undertook tasks central to the maintenance of sovereignty over economic development in the North, as described in Section Two on the trading, whaling, and mining activities in the North.

An indication of the significance of the RCMP to the North is also borne out by the fact that the RCMP commissioner was also commissioner of the NWT from 1905 to 1919. Until 1960 each commissioner of the force was an appointed member of the NWT Council.[88]

The nature of the RCMP's activities in the North today parallels that of the early Klondike days (although the gold is now black) in that their beat ranges mainly from Beaufort Sea exploration camps to the service center, which supports such resource development activities. However, the dog teams are now gone and have been replaced by snowmobiles and Twin Otter aircraft.

JURISPRUDENCE IN THE NORTH

One of the central problems of the RCMP, even today, is recognizing when they must bend the law to fit circumstances specific to the Inuit and aboriginals. Although they are generally expected to uphold laws generated in southern legislatures and courts, experience has taught the RCMP that southern laws sometimes have to be bent to meet northern situations. As a result of this need, constables are now being trained to be sensitive to the aboriginal lifestyles.[89]

A similar trend is also evidenced in modern jurisprudence in the North. In this regard Judge Jack Simmons set a remarkable number of precedents for Inuit jurisprudence. His most memorable case involves Kikkik, a woman who stood trial in 1958 for the murder of her half brother, criminal negligence in the death of her young daughter, and the abandonment of another child. (A description of the extenuating circumstances is included in Appendix 2.) To summarize, the jury found her not guilty mainly because Judge Simmons told them "that justice demanded that they revert to an earlier age and try to understand Kikkik's life, land, and society." I think that this approach was an extraordinarily progressive example of what can be done to accommodate the various interests of multicultural Canada within a tremendous diversity of ethnic pluralism.

THE GEOLOGICAL SURVEY OF CANADA

No other country in the world owes so much to one single agency of government for having explored its land and resources than Canada. Since its inception in 1842, the Geological Survey studied a spectrum of earth science and scanned many allied disciplines as well. This agency took over on land the task that the maritime exploration by the British Navy had left off after the search for Sir John Franklin came to an end. At the time, particularly during the last quarter of the nineteenth century, the officers of the GSC were engaged in a whole natural history survey of parts of Canada that were until then unknown.

As early as the 1870s some officers of the Survey began to penetrate the North, most notably Robert Bell on the east and west side of Hudson Bay to the Latitude of Churchill, just short of 60 degrees.[90] From the 1880s to the early twentieth century, the north-western part of Canada was the exploratory domain of McConnell, Dawson, Bell, Charles Camsell, and Joseph Keele. Other important names responsible for much of the exploration of Northern Saskatchewan and Quebec are Joseph Burr Tyrell and A.P. Low, respectively.

One of the paramount concerns of GSC explorers while in the field was the accumulation of accurate scientific data. With the turn of the century, the nature of the Geological Survey's work changed, and by 1907 "the age of the general observer was past, the day of the giants of geological exploration—men like Dawson, Bell, Tyrell, and McConnell— was substantially ended."[91] To a large extent, this change was a reflection of the attitudes of Reginald Brock, who had come under the directorship of the Survey.

Brock was a nationalist and a firm believer that "Canada's progression to greatness...depended on...the development of its vast mineral wealth."[92] Consequently he insisted on hiring scientists with high standards of technical and academic excellence. In fact Brock instituted a rule requiring all full-time employees of the Survey to have a PhD in their fields. He also instituted the practice of assisting promising PhD candidates with summer employment. This provided the young men with money to finance their studies as well as an opportunity to do field work for their dissertations. Further, most of these young men were later recruited for full-time employment after they graduated.[93]

Brock also moved the Geological Survey towards specialization. In 1908 he created the Topographical Division, which was to provide the geologists with more accurate base maps. His goal was to make the operation more efficient to allow various employees to work in their area of specialization without repeating work. Brock also initiated serious scientific work in the field of ethnology and natural history. Again, only recognized experts were employed to do the work.[94]

As a result of these changes, the nature of the work carried out by the Geological Survey was substantially altered. Up until 1908 single parties had been expected to carry out a broad range of activities, including topographical mapping, geological work, and observations of plant and animal life. Notably the emphasis now shifted to "setting geologists to work intensively in an area of limited size but major economic significance."[95] While work in the Arctic and sub-Arctic was by no means ended, the work was considerably more systemized, and few of the old style expeditions took place.

The post-war years brought further changes for the Geological Survey. Funding to the Mines and Minerals Branch of the Department of Mines grew at the expense of the Survey. This trend began to show itself in a number of ways but became most evident to the Survey when their annual report was included as part of the Department of the Mines' annual report in 1920. In the same year, William Collins was appointed as director of the Survey. Collins was an able administrator and a competent geologist, but he had little interest in the North. Consequently he refused to support reconnaissance expeditions into remote areas for financial and scientific reasons. In part he based his reasoning on the belief that these areas were too isolated to attract the interest of miners and prospectors. Zaslow sums up Collins's attitude this way:

> For many years Collins opposed extending work into the Arctic because of the added expense and the diversion of manpower from what he regarded as more valuable work in more accessible areas.[98]

To a large extent, this approach curtailed the previously well-developed travelling component of the Survey almost entirely. As a result the number of overland travelling expeditions to the Arctic supported by the government was substantially reduced from 1908 onwards. In fact only private individuals such as Ernest Thompson Seton, George Dougal, and James Mitchell-Bullock undertook expeditions similar to reconnaissance expeditions that were inspired by curiosity in the environment.

CONSERVATION

Historically speaking, a glaring omission from the activities of the federal government in the North has been in the area of conservation. Adequate protection of wildlife for future generations has only recently become a policy objective of the federal government. The first formal recognition of the need for conservation in the North extends back to 1914, when the first forest fire program was established along the Lower Slave River.[99] Since that time firefighting services have operated in the North, employing many aboriginal peoples. Unfortunately this well-intentioned program may in fact have been futile. Most northern ecologists agree that boreal forests require a good burning on a fairly regular basis to free needed nutrients, which are often scarce. Furthermore some species, like red pine, have seeds that require a hot fire in order to germinate.

In contrast to the efforts made to protect northern forests, the federal government has never taken as strong of an action to protect endangered animal species. It was not until 1923 that the federal government took any steps to control the fur industry. Five preserves were created in the next fifteen years, with an area of approximately seven hundred and fifteen acres. In addition game sanctuaries were established on Thelon and Twin Islands, covering more than fifteen thousand square miles.[100] These areas afford protection to the muskox which was threatened in the 1920s by the hunting activities of Greenlanders. While other government actions, such as the creation of Wood Buffalo Park, have protected species like the wood bison, their overall effectiveness can be described as limited. In light of the rapid demise of many species, including international stocks of salmon, whales, and caribou, this area will require substantial policy development and the possible assertion of sovereign protection if Canada is to ensure the survival of these species in the future.

Section Four

LEGAL PERSPECTIVES

SOVEREIGNTY AS AN "ISSUE" IN THE 1970S

In the early '70s renewed interest in Canadian sovereignty over the Arctic was seen in the provocative literature that enjoyed national prominence during this period. With provocative titles such as *The Arctic in Question* and *The Arctic Imperative*, authors Dosman and Rohmer stimulated discussions of Arctic sovereignty issues.[101] Dosman suggested that "Canada's hold over its Arctic domain is uncertain," concluding that the Arctic "is the last major region where the territorial integrity of Canada could be challenged."[102] Others such as Granatstein argued that

> *...the lack of concern for the North and the regular and almost automatic acquiescence in American requests since 1942 had eaten away some of Canada's rights. As Canada began to face new and severe challenges in the 1970s, the result seemed to be that the nation had handed away part of its sovereignty.[103]*

Professor Griffiths[104] was more strident:

> *...the Arctic is in real danger of becoming North American without ever having been effectively Canadian...It can only be concluded that Ottawa is determined to surrender out sovereignty piecemeal in a process of national self-immolation.*

In the proliferation of literature that emerged from 1970 to 1975 on Arctic sovereignty, the term "sovereignty" became an abstraction that most academics had difficulty grappling with. In this literature sovereignty is evoked in many different contexts with different meanings. Dosman speaks of northern sovereignty as comprising three elements: (a) public opinions, viewing the issue "with considerable emotion"; (b) pollution control; and (c) Canadian security, broadly defined so as to encompass the safeguarding of strategic resources.[105] Byers expresses concern about sovereignty in the sense of surveillance and control.[106] Langford links sovereignty with "rescue exploitation."[107] Gellner discusses it in terms of what he assesses as a need for "effective occupation"[108] and a greater enforcement capability.[109] Rohmer sees the need for more government involvement as the Arctic imperative.[110] More recently Dyson suggests that sovereignty in the North requires meeting the challenge of the "navigable arctic."[111]

The meaning of the word sovereignty has become so elastic that each renewed use of the word tends to obscure rather than clarify the intent of the authors, assuming that goal is clarification. The ambiguity is not solely the making of the authors. During the stormy period leading up to the Manhattan voyage in 1969, Trudeau stated that "protection of our sovereignty" was Canada's first defense priority. Soon afterward he made an even more ambiguous claim when he argued that "our first priority in our defense policy is the protection of Canadian sovereignty in all dimensions."[112] In addition the 1970 foreign policy review identified "safeguarding sovereignty and independence" as one of the main policy themes for attention by government.[113] In this document sovereignty was associated with a variety of national goals including:

> ...protecting Canada's territorial integrity, its constitutional authority, its national identity, and freedom of action...Above all sovereignty should be used to protect vital Canadian interest and promote Canada's aim and objectives.[114]

Considered in its entirety, government and scholarly literature did much to cloud the issues and stimulate confusing notions. Further, very few of these academics undertook serious study of the problem from a legal perspective, which would have cast their emotional rhetoric and questionable work in an entirely different light.

THE SECTOR THEORY

One approach to delineation of the extent of Canada's claim to Arctic waters and lands was based on the Sector Theory. Sector lines had come into use internationally in 1904 although they were not based on any legal precepts. However, it was not until three years later that the sector approach was applied to the Arctic by Canadian Senator Pascal Poirier:

> ...we can establish a fourth ground for ownership of all the lands and islands that extend from the Arctic Circle up to the North Pole. Last year, I think it was, when our Captain Bernier was in New York, a quest of the Arctic Club, the question being mooted as to the ownership of the Arctic Islands, it was proposed and agreed—and this is not a novel affair—that in future, partition of northern lands, a country whose possession today goes up to the Arctic regions, will have a right, or should have a right, or has the right to all lands that are to be found in the waters between a line extending from its eastern extremity north, and another line extending from the western extremity north. All lands between the two lines up to the North Pole should belong and do belong to the country whose territory abuts up there. Now if we take our geography, it is a simple matter.[115]

Indeed, as Poirier pointed out, it is a novel affair. Margaret Morris explains that the use of meridian lines to clarify sovereignty claims had an extensive history:

> ...As early as 1494, Pope Alexander VI, under the Treaty of Toresillas, separated the colonial territorial claims of Portugal and Spain by lines running from North to South Poles. The Russian-American treaty of 1867, which brought about the sale of Alaska, stated that the dividing lines between Russian and American Territories should proceed "due North without limitation, into the same Frozen Ocean." In 1897, the Dominion order-in-council delimited the Franklin District as all lands and islands between the 141st meridian and Davis Strait. A Department of Interior Map of 1904 showed sector lines running along the 141st and 60th meridians to the North Pole.[116]

While Poirier himself limited his application specifically to "islands and lands" only, others extended his idea to include the whole area confined within the lines of the sector. Thus the problem with the sector approach, as professor Hyde has stated, is that it is indifferent "to the nature of the surface of the areas concerned—whether it be land or ice, or water." Further, it is obvious from the diversity of opinions expressed when Poirier made his proposal that a consensus on the application of the Sector Principle would not (and did not) quickly emerge. Head has summarized the Sector Theory's implications as follows:

> *An Arctic sector is deceptively simple, and is compounded of only two ingredients: a base line of arc described along the Arctic Circle through territory unquestionably within the jurisdiction of a temperate zone state, and sides defined by meridians of longitude, extending from the North Pole south of the most easterly and westerly points on the Arctic Circle priced by the state. Under the theory nations possessing territory extending into the Arctic regions have a rightful claim to all territory—be it land, water or ice—lying to their north. This claim springs from the geographical relationship of claimant state to the claimed territory; the two areas must be contiguous along the Arctic Circles.*[117]

Legal and government authorities responded to the Sector Principle with amazed reactions. Initial response ranged from complete endorsement by a few to expression of considerable doubt by many, while still others firmly refused to concede it had any legal authority.[119] The variety of views expressed among qualified authorities reflects the great variety of state doctrines and practices. As Head points out, opponents of the theory argued powerfully that national claims under the theory were in exact reverse order to the normal process of acquisition. The Sector Theory places territory in legal possession of the state even before it was discovered. How, it was argued, can a state claim sovereignty over areas about which it knows absolutely nothing?[120] Further, Smedel claimed that it gave an unfair advantage to those states bordering the Arctic. "The parties on whom the greatest wrong would be inflicted by the Sector Principle are the states that are not bordered by the Arctic Ocean."[121] Others, such as the Russian theorist Lakhtine[i], spoke in favor of the principle, arguing that "sectors offered the only 'practical' solution to the problem."[122]

Since Poirier's 1907 proposal the Sector Theory's applicability to Canada's North has evolved through various stages, reaching maturity in the views expressed by Professor Pharand in the 1970s.[123] Certainly Poirier's proposal was considered to be premature; his motion was neither seconded nor put to a vote. However, in 1909, Captain Bernier "assembled around Perry's rock to witness the unveiling of a tablet placed on the rock," which read as follows:

> *This memorial is erected today to commemorate the taking possession for the Dominion of Canada of the Whole Arctic Archipelago lying to the north*

of America from longitude 60 degrees West to 141 degrees West up to latitude 90 degrees North.[124]

In retrospect Bernier's enthusiasm was a remarkable expression of concern, although it was virtually ignored by politicians and international lawyers. Today most Canadian officials have relinquished the idea of the Canadian Arctic Sector in favor of a regime of peaceful uses and scientific cooperation in the Polar Basin. The sector notion would probably have been untenable anyway, largely because Canada lacks the military power and political will to make it work in the face of American and Russian Arctic presence. Further, as we will later see, this notion might have had damaging implications for circumpolar cooperation if it had been strictly adhered to by the Canadian government.

TERRITORIAL SOVEREIGNTY IN THE MODERN AGE

International lawyers and international courts have contributed substantially to the literature on the subject of sovereignty. Yet the basic legal definition of sovereignty is a simple one, which has not itself been subject to uncertainty or controversy, although its application to particular fact situations in several parts of the world has often been a matter of controversy between states and between lawyers. The classical statement defining sovereignty over a portion of the globe is perhaps that of Max Huber, the arbitrator in the *Island of Palmas* case, where he referred to it as the "right to exercise therein, to the exclusion of any other state, the functions of a state."[125]

The fact is, as most scholars on Arctic sovereignty acknowledge, that by this definition Canada's legal position as sovereign over the Arctic mainland, islands, and continental shelf was unchallenged by the Manhattan and indeed unchallengeable. The major statement on Arctic sovereignty made by Prime Minister Trudeau into the House of Commons on May 15, 1969, underlined this fact. Further, as noted in a previous section, it has not been disputed by other governments or by a score of legal scholars who have written on the subject in recent years.

Since 1969 two exceptions have come to light, but they are not the focus of the concerns of most authors who have recently questioned Canada's sovereignty in the Arctic. One area where the questions remain, as Frederick[126] explains, is the Canadian/United States maritime boundary area in the Beaufort Sea. Canada has long held that the line of the 141st meridian of west longitude established by the 1825 treaty between Great Britain and Russia forms not only the land border (which is undisputed) but also the seaward extension of the border. Canada has granted continental shelf exploration permits up to that line. The United States, on the other hand, has taken the view that the maritime boundary departs from the meridian and runs in a north-easterly direction along the median or equidistance line between the United States and Canadian coasts. The differing views of the two governments came into sharp focus in November 1976 when the United States anticipated Canada's extension of its fisheries jurisdiction. Canada immediately indicated that it did not accept this line (and others).

Presently this question is under the scrutiny of a United States-Canada Joint Commission on Maritime Boundaries. In a recent article, Dosman and Abele have reviewed some issues related to offshore diplomacy in the Beaufort Sea.[127] They suggest that External Affairs may sacrifice the undisputed area for concessions in the Gulf of Maine. Unfortunately this strategy might, in fact, be a mistake. Although the area itself is relatively small, it is located in shallow waters and could prove valuable in the study of seabed geology (Refer to Figure 1).

The other exception to the unquestioned status of Canadian sovereignty over its northern territories is a minor one. It relates to Hans Island, a small, uninhabited island less than one mile long lying between Greenland and Ellesmere Island in Nares Strait, at latitude 80 degrees 49 minutes North and claimed by both Canada and Greenland.[127] The fact that there were differing views on who owned the island did not come to light until 1971, when Canadian and Danish officials noticed discrepancies in the course of negotiations on continental shelf boundary delimitation in this area. At the time Denmark and Canada were unable to reach an agreement and decided instead to simply ignore Hans Island. Since the island happens to straddle the median line between Greenland and Ellesmere Island, it was decided to draw the continental shelf boundary up to a low water mark on the south end of the island and resume the boundary again from the low water mark on the north end. The island thus appears as a gap in the geographical coordinates listed in the Canada/Denmark Maritime Boundary Delimitation Agreement signed on December 17, 1973. This agreement had the effect of denying, for all practical purposes, any jurisdiction over contiguous waters and continental shelf to whatever party eventually is able to sustain its claim to the island. The only problem that remains, therefore, is the question of title to the rock itself, which appears to be of little interest to either side from the viewpoint of habitation or resource development.[128]

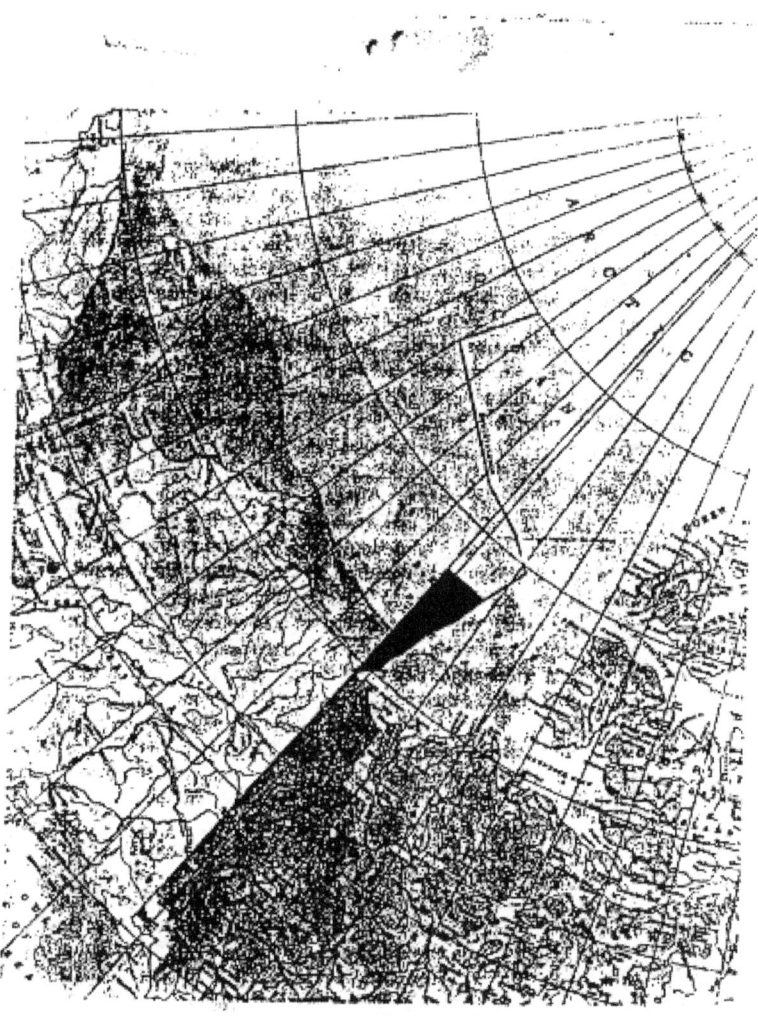

Figure 1. Map of the Beaufort Sea showing the
zone of the Continental Shelf in question. The
Canadian government has claimed the Shelf to the
141st meridian while the U.S. government is ap-
plying the equidistant argument. From M. Frederick
" La delimitation du Plateau Continental entre le
Canada et L'Etats-Unis dans La mer de Beaufort ",
Canadian Yearbook of International Law 1979, pp.
30-96.

EFFECTIVE OCCUPATION

A belief that was popularized in the '70s, after the emotional Manhattan incident, was that in order to maintain a sovereign title in the North, it was imperative that Canada undertake more government activity, almost for its own sake. The call for "effective occupation" and "presence" in the Arctic blurred the legal importance of this concept. An examination of the rules of international laws governing claims to sovereignty suggest that effective occupation takes on a much different character in the North.

The leading case and principal source of legal doctrine is the Eastern Greenland case decided by the Permanent Court of International Justice in 1933.[129] This precedent would be directly relevant to any dispute over Canadian Arctic territories. In the case the court was called upon to decide on competing claims by Norway and Denmark to sovereignty over Eastern Greenland, in circumstances where each side was able to bring evidence showing that at various times it had laid claim to this remote, uninhabited area. The court upheld Denmark's claim on the grounds that although its authority had been exercised only intermittently, it nevertheless constituted effective occupation in the circumstances. Reviewing previous cases, the court stated that in disputes over territorial sovereignty:

> *In many cases the tribunal has been satisfied with very little in the way of the actual exercise of sovereign rights, provided that the other state could not make out a superior claim. This is particularly true in the case of claims to sovereignty over areas in thinly populated or unsettled countries.*[130]

An earlier judicial precedent for the same principle of international law is the *Clipperton Island Arbitration* between France and Mexico in 1931[131] in which France was recognized as sovereign over the uninhabited island, despite the fact that France was unable to show that it had exercised any authority or act of sovereignty on the island for twenty-nine years—from 1858 to 1887. However, no other state had done so either, and the arbitrator held that over a more extended period of time, and by reason of original occupation, France's claim was superior to Mexico's.

It is clear from the above examples that those who preach activism in the North for its own sake are misguided if they base themselves on a belief that international law requires a high level of activity in uninhabited Arctic areas. "Effective occupation" is important to any claim of sovereignty, but in sparsely settled regions the level of state activity may be very modest and intermittent, as long as it is more than that exercised by any other competing state. Thus the enormous range of domestic activities that have been undertaken in recent years have substantially increased Canada's potential for claiming effective occupation of the land and waters of the Arctic.[133] In fact, as Dobell suggests, the regular Department of National Defence "sovereignty flights" to the high Arctic could probably be cut back without prejudice to Canadian claims to sovereignty in the Arctic.[134] Here most international lawyers would agree, I suspect, because the activity should be judged in terms of its functional purpose.

LAW OF SEA AND MULTILATERAL NEGOTIATIONS

The issue of jurisdiction over the Arctic waters came to the fore once again with the discovery of oil at Prudhoe Bay in Alaska and the extensive exploration for discovery of oil and gas in the Canadian high Arctic. International law in this area is generally unclear, and in some cases the principles and bilateral agreements that have settled previous disputes were viewed in the early 1970s as inappropriate by the Canadian government. Thus the Canadian government was forced to take independent action and develop new theories of international law in relation to the special problems of jurisdiction over its Arctic waters.

The main pressure to implement special provisions that would protect its Arctic waters was the sailing of the *Manhattan* through the North West Passage. After futile attempts to achieve multilateral agreements between the United States and the Canadian government in 1969, the federal government saw fit to enlarge the definition of innocent passage and, more specifically, to clarify the concept and make it more relevant to the Arctic in order to protect Canada's interests.[135] In view of the possibility of ecological damage to areas such as Lancaster Sound and the threat to Canadian sovereignty, the federal government felt it could not recognize the passage of foreign ships in the Arctic as innocent. An almost immediate response from Ottawa was to extend its offshore boundary to the twelve mile limit applied by many other countries at the time to protect their fish stocks.[136] Soon after this the government enacted legislation to further protect the Arctic waters, which was called the Arctic Waters Pollution Prevention Act.

Appendix Two

The trial of Kikkik by Justice Sissons.
(extracted from Canada's North Today.
Ministry of Supply and Services: Ottawa, 1978.)

Flying in rough bush aircraft in the worst of weather, Justice Sissons did bring the judicial system to the native people. He unabashedly admitted being in the front lines for the struggle over native rights and for more responsible government in the North. He bent the law to embrace different cultures and some of his rulings went before the Supreme Court of Canada. To the Inuit he became known as Ekoktoegee, The One Who Listens To Things.

Justice Sissons tried many important cases but one gives a brief and valuable insight into life and justice North of 60. That is the case of Kikkik, who stood trial in 1958 for the murder of her half-brother, for criminal negligence in the death of her young daughter and for abandonment of another child.

Kikkik and her family were Ihalmiut, inland Inuit, from the Ennadai Lake area of the central barrens not far north of the Manitoba-Saskatchewan borders. Her family and that of her half-brother Ootuk were caught out on the barrens with little food. Ootuk, for reasons not yet totally understood, shot Hallow, Kikkik's husband. Kikkik then fatally stabbed Ootuk.

Widowed and without food, Kikkik tried to guide her five children across the snows to a Hudson's Bay Post 64 kilometers away. After eight days on the trail she left two of the children in an igloo. Before rescue came, one child, age three died.

At the murder trial, defence counsel Sterling Lyon, now Manitoba premier, argued that the only conclusion Kikkik could have drawn was that Ootuk also planned to kill her and her children. Justice Sissons told the jury that justice demanded that they

revert to an earlier age and try to understand Kikkik's life, land and society.

The verdict was not guilty, but Kikkik then had to stand trial on the other two charges.

Kikkik had abandoned her two children on the morning of the day she was rescued. They were still alive in the igloo but she said they had died during the night. Rescuers sent to find the bodies found one of the children still alive.

Kikkik's explanation was short and simple. The children could not walk and she had dragged them a long way. She did not tell the rescuers they were alive because she was afraid.

Justice Sissons said later the excuse would not be good enough in white society. But Inuit society was vastly different and Kikkik probably was genuinely afraid that she would be punished for revealing that she had abandoned two children in hopes of saving the others.

The jury found her not guilty on both counts.

These actions gained informal support by Stockholm in 1972 at the Conference on the Environment when delegates endorsed a statement of objectives that recognized the particular interests of coastal states with respect to the management of their resources.[137]

Unfortunately the United States did not accept Canada's unilateral declaration of a twelve mile territorial sea in 1970 or the right of the Canadian government to assert "functional" sovereignty over the Arctic waters as a pollution control measure.[138] Given its military, geopolitical, economic and related global maritime's interests, the United States is intensely concerned about the right of free passage through international straits, obviously this also includes the North West Passage.

Although the North West Passage does link two bodies of "high seas" and therefore could be defined as an international strait, Canada denied it had this status because it is not used for international navigation, but this is a weak argument in view of the probability that powerful icebreakers will be able to traverse Arctic waters without difficulty. In 1981 Dey[139] reviewed shipping routes and ice cover in Arctic waters and suggested that with the aid of remote sensing technology and computer simulations, it would be possible by the late 1980s to conduct year-round successful shipping of hydrocarbons. To this end, Pharand has reviewed the status of the North West Passage in international law and he concludes with these propositions.

By way of summing up, seven main propositions may be formulated. (1) The North West Passage is a legal strait, in that there is an overlap of territorial waters in Barrow Strait and Prince of Wales Strait and the right of innocent passage applies. (2) The North West Passage is not an international strait, since it has never been used for international investigation, and the right of innocent passage is suspendable. (3) Preparations are being made to transport hydrocarbons year-round and, unless Canada imposes and enforces appropriate conditions on foreign users, the Northwest passage might well become an international strait in a relatively short time. (4) If the Northwest Passage becomes an international strait the presently applicable right of innocent passage will become non-suspendable under existing law (Territorial Sea Convention of 1958) and the new right of transit passage becomes applicable to the Northwest Passage, ships and aircraft will enjoy a right of passage in their normal mode, including the submerged passage of submarines. (6) Notwithstanding the applicability of transit passage to the North West Passage, Canada would retain the right to establish and enforce regulations for the prevention of marine pollution, such as those presently existing under the Arctic Pollution Prevention Act of 1970. The validity of this act has been confirmed internationally by the insertion of a special provision for "ice-covered area" in the I.N.N.T. and under the text as it presently exists, those special powers of the coastal state would continue to apply. (7) If Canada does not develop year-round icebreaking and navigational capability, as well as oil-spill monitoring and clean-up technology, its control over the North West Passage might well become nominal and irreversible damage to the ecological balance of the marine environment might result.[140]

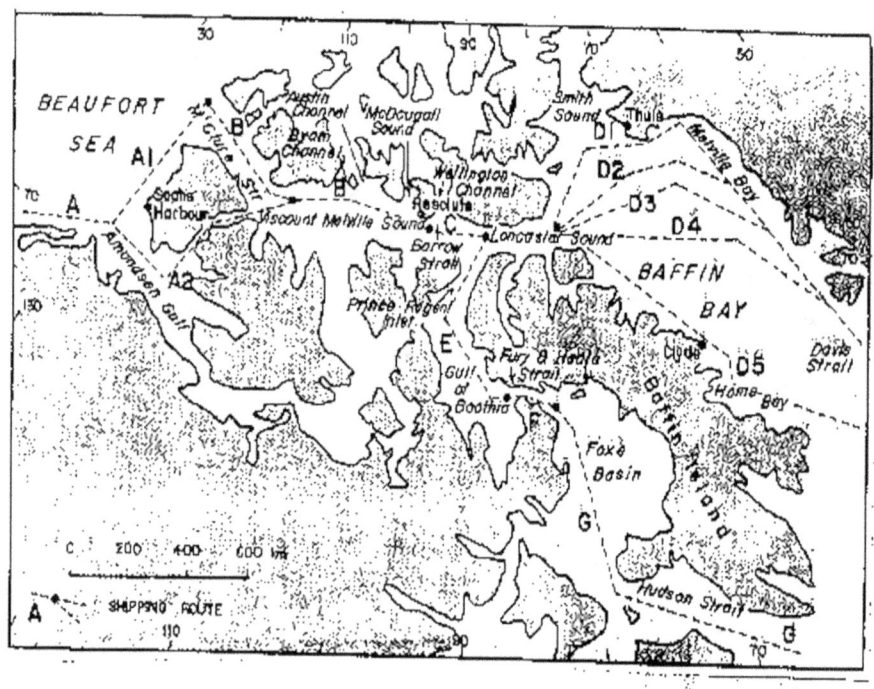

Figure 2.   Possible Year-round shipping Routes in the Canadian Arctic. From Balaram B. Dey, " Shipping Routes, Ice Cover and Year-Round Navigation in the Canadian Arctic " Polar Record, Vol. 20 No. 129(1981), pp. 549-59.

Thus it seems fairly clear that the one significant gap in Canadian sovereignty is the North West Passage. Evan Browne[141] has echoed this concern in a recent article; the solution that he and many others advocate is pragmatic. Canada should substantially increase investment in ice-breaking technology. The key question that this pragmatic solution raises is what the cost will be to develop this technology and others. Canada seems to be adopting a "wait and see stance," as Browne points out.[142] Unfortunately this could have serious long-term implications for Canadian sovereignty in the future. While the "development for effective occupation" argument might not sit well with me, this is one area where Canada *must* keep pressing at the United Nations Convention on Law of the Sea (UNCLOS) conference for multilateral support for its interests. Mestral and Legault[143] suggest that Canada can defend its interests and promote them effectively at UNCLOS provided that:

1. The interests are perceived to be truly important by other delegations at UNCLOS,
2. Delegations to UNCLOS for Canada know what they are seeking, and
3. The delegations have strong support from the Canadian government and strong internal unity.

"To broaden this support and consolidate this unity, it is important to keep the public informed and to ensure active participation in the delegation by a wide range of government departments as well as by parliamentary representatives from both sides of the House of Common, provincial representatives, and also representatives from the most immediately affected socio-economic interest groups."[144]

While these basic requirements will be difficult to fulfill, they would certainly improve Canada's opportunity to assert sovereign control of the North West Passage and/or some form of pollution control in this area.

Section Five

THE CIRCUMPOLAR NORTH

THE CONCEPT OF CIRCUMPOLARITY

"A glance at the map of the Northern Hemisphere shows that the Arctic Ocean is in effect a huge Mediterranean," Vilhjalmur Steffansson wrote in 1922.[144] The concept was somewhat novel at the time because it was by no means clear how a frozen ocean could bring together rather than divide the lands around its shore. Since that time technology has borne out Steffansson's predictions that those in a hurry to go from England to Japan "will fly over the North polar oceans."[145] Further, the development of nuclear-powered ice-breakers has altered our perspective on the impermeability of the Arctic Ocean. In 1977 the *Arkitca*, a Soviet ice-breaker, reached the North Pole.[146] The wedding of technology and geography has given rise to two questions:

1. To what extent has the relative ease of contract between the countries around the North Pole affected political and economic relations between those countries in the Circumpolar North and with the rest of the world?
2. Is a sense of community developing in the North as a result?

The answer to these questions will be examined in relation to Canadian sovereignty in the Circumpolar North. In addition the importance of cultural exchange, technological transfer, and environmental protection in the Circumpolar North will be explored.

THE GEOGRAPHY OF CIRCUMPOLAR CULTURE

When one examines the Circumpolar North, one cannot help but recognize that it is best described as an ocean surrounded almost completely by a ring of land, the only substantial break being between Greenland and Scandinavia. The other breaks are the relatively minor straits between the Canadian Archipelago and the ninety-kilometer gap between Asia and America, the Bering Strait (Refer to Figure 3). There are also strong similarities between physical and geophysical features, climate, and the fauna and flora of the circumpolar nations. In addition regions of permafrost, tundra, and taiga are distributed throughout the landmasses on all sides of the ocean. [147]

Perhaps more significantly, from social and political viewpoints, is the shared cultural heritage of northern residents. Modern Western societies entered the northern lands in two major movements, northward and westward across the North Atlantic, and then across the North American continent, and northward and eastward from Russia across the Eurasian continent, both movements meeting the North Pacific and Alaska. Thus, Inuit, for example, are distributed in roughly similar bands ranging from eastern Siberia across Alaska and Canada into Greenland, a fact that motivated the Inuit to hold a number of conferences on circumpolar problems during the recent past.[148]

These conferences have specifically been directed at problems raised by Western-oriented development in the Circumpolar North. The world of circumpolar peoples is changing rapidly. Economic growth is spearheading these changes, while social and political development are playing important secondary roles. Under such dynamic circumstances, adaptation—by both northern peoples and southern developers—is essential, and such adaptation means open and meaningful discussions of proposed developments and involvement in actual undertakings. Otherwise confrontation and seemingly endless and often needless, bitter wrangling will haunt southern development projects. Thus, in my opinion, sensible development in the Circumpolar North will require an understanding of the relation between northern people and industrial society and their roles and positions in modern nations. If this philosophical view is to be embraced, then it will necessitate the sharing of experiences and information between northern peoples. Further, the place of northerners in Western society must be examined in relation to conservation and destruction of traditional culture. Those cultures that have experienced assimilation in the Old World North and the USSR can provide North American northern aboriginal peoples with insight into the effects of modernization and economic development. The problem of maintenance and protection of the traditional cultures of ethnic minorities inhabiting these areas is only one small example of the problem that circumpolar exchanges between northern peoples can mitigate.

SCIENTIFIC CO-OPERATION AND TECHNOLOGY TRANSFER

International science has been moving forward on many fronts, often with UNESCO support, but not in the Arctic. Although much of the Circumpolar North shares similar climatological, geographical, hydrological, floral, and faunal conditions, the sparseness of population and lack of attraction to scientists has, historically speaking, de-emphasized scientific development in the North.[149]

International cooperation in polar science got a good and early start in the discussions that led to the International Polar Year of 1882–1883. Armstrong [150] described it:

> The value of this co-operative effort was attested by the decision, taken shortly after the Second World War, that the next Polar Year should be held twenty-five rather than fifty years after the previous one, and it should be widened to cover the whole world. The International Geophysical Year of 1957–1958, in which sixty-seven nations worked together, grew out of the International Polar Years. After the International Geophysical Year ended, the International Council of Scientific Unions established a Scientific Committee on Antarctic Research to continue the scientific cooperation in the Antarctic carried out at the time.

Due to the greater significance of the North in strategic terms, no organization corresponding to the Scientific Committee on Antarctic

Research has emerged in the Arctic. Further, in the case of the USSR, the whole of the North is denied to visitors from the West, and much scientific information has been withheld. This has been and remains the greatest stumbling block to full international scientific collaboration in the North. [151]

One of the most progressive documents issued in relation to scientific cooperation in the North has been issued by the Canadian government.[152] The guidelines draw attention to the need for Canada to assist international scientific projects while obviously maintaining a strong commitment to Canadian objectives. "Such guidelines should go a long way in preventing misunderstandings and in removing what could become a source of difficulty in international cooperation, especially when nations of different sizes and capabilities are involved."[153] Let us hope that they open northern Canada to foreign scientists in the future, and that it becomes practiced in all northern countries some day.

DEFENCE IN THE CIRCUMPOLAR NORTH

For many years it has been assumed that the Arctic and sub-Arctic regions could be a theater of warfare between the United States and the Soviet Union. Interest in Arctic defense materialized from the realization that most industrial nations capable of supporting a war were north of the 60th parallel of the north latitude. Of growing concern is the increase in Russia's military presence in the Northeast Atlantic, a problem which has been raised by many authors. One response suggested by Griffiths is that Canada should play a more active role in NATO defense of Norway and Iceland.[154]

Another proposal which would be far more radical but much more sensible in the long run would be creating a demilitarized zone in the Arctic. Hanna Newcombe has proposed a nuclear-free zone in the Arctic.[155] As she points out, the world has had a disarmed and inspected zone in Antarctica since 1959. The twelve nations concerned have territorial claims and have even disputed these claims, but the treaty has held. In theory this success could be extended to the Arctic, where the possibilities of an armed conflict are more serious. Since Canada is an important Arctic power, it would be fitting for Canada to propose this alternative. A demilitarized zone in which there are no military weapons of any kind, nuclear or conventional; no military personnel, equipment, or bases would be ambitious to implement. However, a less ambitious scheme that would "make the Arctic a nuclear-free zone" could be adopted as a start. While there are serious problems to be solved if such a proposal is to be instituted, the ultimate benefits would be substantial.

THE CIRCUMPOLAR OCEANS

One of the main reasons why a new framework for foreign policy-making must be divided for the Arctic is the potential impact of marine technology on scientific research and exploration. In the context of fisheries, new technologies have radically increased the world fishing effort and rendered previous international fisheries organizations helpless in controlling catch limits and enforcing conservation regulations. The development of large mobile factory fleets, particularly by the Soviet Union and Japan, has made it possible for countries to maintain bases at considerable distances from their port of origin. Since recognition of the two hundred-mile EEZ by UNCLOS seems inevitable, Canada is virtually assured that this will not be a major problem for fisheries in the Arctic Archipelago in the future.[156] However, as previously pointed out, some species such as the salmon on the east coast have been depleted in the past.

Technological advances in exploration and exploitation of oil, gas, and other resources in commercial quantities, considerably beyond previously known limits, have serious implications for the circumpolar oceans. These issues cannot be ignored. The prospect of rich, offshore resources has encouraged many circumpolar nations to show a growing interest in their northern continental shelves.[157] Previously these areas had been only of limited economic and scientific interest, and very little is known as a result. As Dunbar points out, Canadian data on oceanography, hydrology, and archipelagic ecology is so sparse that the deficiencies raise doubts about our ability to develop offshore mineral resources.[158] This, in fact, is an excellent example of an area where scientific cooperation could be naturally beneficial in the Arctic.

Marine environmental issues have, within the last two decades, come to receive considerable attention. Since the 1960 Geneva UNCLOS, the number of international marine environmental conventions has steadily grown to cover such aspects as land-based sources of pollution and dumping pollution from ships. Nevertheless the gap between the purpose of such conventions and international practice remains wide, which is most clearly illustrated through the continuing large-scale oil pollution from vessels. A succession of tanker accidents since the *Torrey Canyon* and blow out incidents such as *Ekofisk* in the North Sea and *Ixtoc* in the Gulf of Mexico have served to dramatize the environmental issues at stake. They have also highlighted the related problems of poorly enforced conventions and the technical difficulties in dealing with large oil spills, as well as human error.[159]

Such concerns find expression in a lengthy draft article in the negotiating text of UNCLOS, which could give Canada regulatory powers to designate special areas, such as Lancaster Sound, within the EEZ as vulnerable to pollution for ecological and oceanographic reasons.[160] Such areas would be subject to international approval by competent international organizations. In addition the text contains a provision, again largely at Canadian insistence, that allows coastal states to establish non-discriminatory regulations within the EEZ in order to reduce the likelihood for major pollution damage in certain ecologically vulnerable ice-covered areas such as may be found in the Arctic.[161]

Another major reason that a more coherent foreign policy must be developed for the North is the increasing military uses of the ocean. For the major naval powers, the development of submarine-launched ballistic missiles has meant an enhanced interest in strategic sea routes, long-rang operations, and the acquisition of naval intelligence. At the Law of the Sea Conference, these factors have been at least one of the main sets of considerations shaping the approach of the major naval powers to such questions as access through straits for civil and military vessels and the freedom to conduct marine scientific research.[162] Since the 1970s conventional naval power has become more important as a means of establishing claims to and monitoring maritime boundaries, as well as in minor power conflicts. In the Arctic naval forces have been used most strikingly by the Soviet Union to project Soviet power through the acquisition of bases and ports and the development of an extensive ocean fleet in the region. Dyson says that, in comparison, Canada has a very poor network of tankers, ice-breakers, and ocean ports, a serious problem in the far North for future developments.[163]

In reality the legal uncertainties that have been the subject of debate at UNCLOS during the past decade are probably only the meager beginnings of an ongoing debate about usage of the Arctic oceans. Future developments in these three main areas—security, threats to the marine environment, and the search for resources—will also make it likely that maritime issues remain significant sources of international tension. As already noted, the increased use of the sea for a wide variety of foreign policy and security purposes will enhance interest in maritime-derived intelligence, marine scientific research, and the capability to deploy in order to deter, beat, or defeat other actors. One can anticipate that issues connected with access, for example, through territorial seas and straits, seabed installations, acoustic detection, and the acquisition of maritime states with Arctic oil may necessitate the development of heavily-used tanker routes. Environmentally safe transport of goods through the Arctic will undoubtedly require great cooperation between nations, and accidental spills will require a quick, unified response. Finally recent technological developments in, for example, offshore installation design, artificial islands, ocean data acquisition systems, and sensing of the earth's resources by satellites are beginning to extend significantly the range of civil and military exploration and inquiry undertaken by northern nations. These developments will no doubt generate new, and at times critical, issues for circumpolar nations in the Arctic.

THE END OF SOVEREIGNTY: THE TECHNOLOGICAL HORIZON

History and technology have had quite different effects on national sovereignty. The historical process has accentuated and perpetuated the autonomy of sovereign states. In the past when a state surrendered its sovereignty, defeated by conquest or overrun by revolution, it was only a transfer of sovereignty. However, to a certain degree, modern technology renders national sovereignty in a different light. Revolutions in communications and increased multinational power have created a world in which the sharing of sovereignty is essential for the survival of the human species. As long as the level of operational integration remains less than the area encompassing the problem, we will not find solutions to international problems. While I am not naive enough to suggest the end of sovereignty, which is rooted in economic social, cultural, and political realities, I think that the future of sovereignty will be quite different from its past.

TOWARDS AN INTEGRATED POLICY RESPONSE

Integrated and appropriate solutions to the complex problems of security, technology, aboriginal self-government, cultural development, and environmental protection require a new approach to policy-making. In organizational terms this may mean that an advisory committee on northern development should be revitalized under inter-ministerial control to oversee such policy matters. However, at a theoretical level a more important principle is implied: meta-policy-making.[167] The following quote suggests the meaning of the term meta-policy-making in this context:

> *Policy-making, in the larger sense of the term, includes three main states: (a) meta-policy-making, that is, policy-making on how to make policy; (b) policy-making in its usual sense, that is, making policy on substantive issues; and (c) re-policy-making, that is, making changes in policy based on feedback from the executing policies. A comprehensive optimal model must include these three states, which are dynamically interrelated. The distinction between them is often relative, though it is real; the same stage may, from the point of view of a higher level, be an executing of policy, whereas, from the point of view of a lower level, it may be meta-policy-making. Therefore even though a policy-making system involves many stages and levels, this triple-stage structure of the model includes all of them.[168]*
>
> *The meta-policy-making phases manage the policy-making system as a whole. Or at least manage significant sections of it. They (a) identify problems, values, and resources, and allocate them to different policy-making units; (b) design, evaluate, and redesign the policy-making system; and (c) determine the policy-making strategies. They are a very important part of the optimal model, especially because they are neglected in most normative models. Thanks to them (and to the feedback phases), the model can be used to analyze, evaluate, and improve the policy-making system as a dynamic system, rather than as a collection of separate policy-making unites and cases.*

The implications of this approach are twofold. In the first instance, the meta-policy-making process requires constant planning, research, and review of all three levels of policy making. In the second, definition of values, objectives, and human and financial resources, particularly in relation to the goals of northern development, becomes problematic.

Previous refusals on the part of the federal government to delineate the role of meta-policy-making processes have prevented many agencies from forming meaningful policies towards northern development, as I have already pointed out. Fragmented legislative structures require that projects such as the Arctic Pilot Project must pass through approximately thirty-six regulatory structures at considerable cost to the taxpayer, although it will probably never be evaluated in terms of a clearly enunciated northern policy.

The absence of a clear strategy in foreign policy is also reflected in the dispute evolving between Greenland and Canada over the Arctic Pilot Project.[169] In the interest of diplomacy and international peace, the interrelatedness between what is done internally by a nation and what transpires outside of that nation due to its foreign policy must be recognized. While harnessing and integrating the energies of the Department of External Affairs with various internally oriented ministries will prove difficult, it may, in fact, be the most important challenge to Canada in the assertion of Arctic sovereignty in the next decade. However, in historical perspective, this is a small obstacle in light of what has already been achieved.

CONCLUSION

This book has reviewed the evolution of Canadian sovereignty in the Arctic during the past century. Canada's sovereignty over the North, as reflected in the policy-making activities of the federal government, the administration of northern peoples, and the history of resource development in the region, is a gradual progression from an incoherent and uncoordinated approach, to internal and external problems, to a more integrated and judicious approach.

Nevertheless some problem areas persist. The needs of northerners remain, even today, poorly integrated into policy-making activities. Meanwhile the recent acceleration of development activities in the North has emphasized the need to promote the emergence of national and ethnic identities, both Canadian and abroad. I would advocate a strengthening of ties between indigenous peoples in the polar North, sharing Griffith's belief that this linkage "expresses in constructive fashion the *northerness* of Canada's Inuit and Métis and pursues human rights objectives that would be supported by the Canadian government."[164] [emphasis added]

In addition to encouraging cultural exchange, environmental protection policies should be integrated at an international and national level. On a national level, Lucas has reviewed the nature of the extensive regulatory system now in place to monitor and control marine operations in northern Canada. He concludes that many significant gaps in policy persist, mainly in relation to the lack of mandatory process for public review and the absence of integrated planning.[165] Further, fragmentation of authority seriously discourages thorough assessment of proposals and inhibits the ability of agencies to pursue particular regulatory objectives. Dosman and Abele[166] echo this and suggest that the fears many Canadian environmentalists struggled with in the 1970s concerning policy disintegration could become a reality in the '80s.

The international problem is of no less significance, however. Most evidence suggests that pollution knows no boundaries. Thus solutions to acid rain and oil spills require international cooperation. Unfortunately this prescription, which might be called the ecological imperative, fundamentally contradicts economic, political, and national imperatives. In contrast to the nature of economics of nationalism, the basic principle of ecology is indivisibility. This is why any solutions to environmental problems that are worked out must be circumpolar by definition. The difficulties that Canadians witnessed with the UNCLOS process in the early 1980s bode ill for the future of environmental preservation in the North. False pride and a jealously guarded and carelessly implemented sovereignty in the North will prove anti-ecological and will reinforce differences in economic development and environmental quality in the Circumpolar North, to the detriment of all northern nations.

APPENDIX 1

MAJOR EARLY EXPEDITIONS IN THE ARCTIC REGION[1]

Captain	Region Explored	Date
Frobisher	Baffin Island	1576
Greely		1881-1884
Sir John Franklin	Baffin Island and the Arctic Islands	
W. Wakeham	Hudson Strait	1897
A.P. Low	Hudson Bay and the Arctic Islands	1903-1904
J. Bernier	General	1906-1911
O. Sverdrup	Axel Heiberg, the Elf Ringnes and Amund Ringnes or the "Sverdrup" Islands	1891 - 1902
Macmillan and Byrd	Ellesmere Island	1925

[1] As a general rule, most of the British Royal Navy expeditions are not included because they were not considered major and were more in the realm of regular excursions in support of the Canadian Colony. In addition, some of the smaller expeditions by British-born explorers including John Hornby, R.H. Patterson, Gordon Matthews, Cosmo Melville and Philipp Godsell and America-born traders, explorers and adventurers such as the Douglas Brothers are not included.

APPENDIX 2

CHRONOLOGY OF EVENTS

1880 – Arctic Islands Order in Council proclaims Canadian sovereignty over all British territories in North America.

1969 – Voyage of U.S. tanker *S.S. Manhattan* through the Northwest Passage.

1970 – Canada passes the Arctic Waters Pollution Prevention Act, declaring Canadian regulatory control over pollution within a 100-mile zone.

1973 – Canada and Denmark agree on "delimitation of the continental shelf" between Greenland and Canada.

1985 – Voyage of U.S. icebreaker *CGS Polar Sea* through the Northwest Passage.

1985 – Government of Canada announces plans to acquire "Polar 8 icebreaker."

1987 – Canada's 1987 White Paper on Defence announces plans to acquire 10-12 nuclear submarines.

1988 – Canada and United States reach an agreement on "Arctic Cooperation," which pledges that voyages of U.S. icebreakers should seek consent from Canada.

2000 – Government of Canada releases The Northern Dimension of Canada's Foreign Policy, including policy of asserting Canadian sovereignty in the North.

2003 – Canada ratifies United Nations Convention on the Law of the Sea (UNCLOS).

2004 – Arctic Climate Impact Assessment (Arctic Council) is released.

2004 – Speech from the Throne, announcing a "northern strategy."

2005 – Canada's Minister of National Defence visits Hans Island in July.

2005 – A U.S. nuclear submarine voyages to the North Pole in December, possibly travelling through Canadian Arctic waters. Canada completes delimitation of the continental shelf as part of UNCLOS.

Source: Based in part on a chronology that appeared in Canada, Library of Parliament, Canadian Arctic Sovereignty, PRB 05-61E, January 26, 2006.

BIBLIOGRAPHY

Alcock, F.J. "Albert Peter Low," *The Canadian Geographical Journal*. Vol. 38 (4): 160-63 (April 1954).

Armstrong, T.E. "The Strategic Significance of the Canadian Arctic." In *The Arctic Frontier*, edited by R. St. J. Macdonald, 262-65. Toronto: University of Toronto Press, 1966.

Bernier, J.E. *Report on the Dominion Government Expedition to the Arctic Islands, etc., 1906-07*, 192-95. Ottawa: Kings Printer, 1910. Quoted in Morris Zaslow, *The Opening of the Canadian North 1870-1914*. Toronto: McClelland and Stewart Ltd., 1971: 267.

Brant, Charles S. and Charles W. Hobart. "Eskimo Education, Danish and Canadian: A Comparison," *The Canadian Review of Sociology and Anthropology*, Vol. 2: 47-66 (May 1966).

Brody, Hugh. *The Peoples Land*. Markham: Penguin, 1975.

Browne, Evan. "Sovereignty Questions remain after Century in the Arctic," *International Perspectives*, p. 7-11 (July/August 1980).

Bryers, R.B. "Sovereignty and Canadian Foreign Policy: the Need for Enforcement Capability." In *The Arctic in Question*, edited by E.J. Dosman, 58-84. Toronto: Oxford University Press, 1976.

Butler, W.E. *International straits of the World: Northeast Arctic passage*. Alphen aan Rijn: Sijthoff & Noordhoff, 1978.

Canada. *Explanatory Note from Colonial Minister Joseph Chamberlin attached to the Colonial Boundaries Act* (July 26, 1895). Quoted in Gordon W. Smith, 14. "Canada's Arctic Archipelago: 100 Years of Canadian Jurisdiction, Part I: The Transfer." *North/Nord* (Spring 1980), 14.

Canada. Imperial Order in Council. July 3, 1880. Quoted in Gordon W. Smith "Canada's Arctic Archipelago: 100 Years of Canadian Jurisdiction, Part I: The Transfer." North/Nord (Spring 1980), 11.

Canada. Senate. Debates, 1906-1907. p. 271. Quoted in Margaret W. Norris, "Boundary Problems Relating to the Sovereignty of the Canadian Arctic," The Musk-Ox No. 6: 54 (1969).

Canada. 1974. *The James Bay Treaty Series No.9.* (made in 1905 and 1906 and adhesions made in 1929 and 1930).

Canada, Department of Defence, *Foreign Policy for Canadians*, Ottawa: Queens Printer, 1970.

Canada, Department of Foreign Affairs and International Trade [DFAIT], "Canada and Denmark Issue Statement on Hans Island," News release, 19 September 2005.

Canada, Department of Indian Affairs and Northern Development, *Canada's North Today*, Ottawa: Supplies and Services,1978: 28-29.

Caswell, John E. "The Sponsors of Canadian Arctic Exploration: 1844-1859," *The Beaver*, Outfit 300: 45-53 (Winter, 1969).

Clemens, W. "Ecology and International Relations," *International Journal*, Vol. 28: 1-28 (Winter 1972-1973).

Cookie, A. and C. Holland. The Exploration of Northern Canada: 500 to 1920, A Chronology Toronto: Arctic History Press, 1978.

Cummings, P., and N.Y. Mickenburg. Native Rights in Canada. Toronto: General Publishing, 1972.

Balaram B. Dey, Shipping routes, ice cover and year-round navigation in the Canadian Arctic, Polar Record Vol. 20 (129): 549-559, 1981.

Past forecasts by geologists of potentially large oil and natural gas reserves in the North American Arctic (eg, Prudhoe Bay, the Mackenzie delta, and the Canadian Arctic islands) are coming closer to reality. Results from Canmar (Canadian Marine Drilling Ltd of Calgary) drill ships working in the southern Beaufort Sea continue to support the prediction of considerable hydrocarbon deposits in this area. The most significant discovery, gas amounting to 0.48–0.50 trillion m3 [17–18 trillion ft3] was made by Panarctic Oils Limited in the Canadian High Arctic, in particular the Drake field off Melville Island and the surrounding region (Star Phoenix, 1980a). Panarctic Oils is a government-industry consortium; Petro-Canada owns 45 per cent of the shares and provides the bulk of the exploration budget.

Day, Balaran. "Shipping Routes, Ice Cover and Year-Round Navigation in the Canadian Arctic,"

Dear, Michael. "Planning Community Health Services in Arctic Canada," The Musk-Ox No. 19: 28-36 (1976).

Dobel, "The Policy Dimension." In *The Arctic in Question*, edited by E.J. Dosman, 121-139. Toronto: Oxford University Press, 1976.

Dosman, E.J., ed., *The Arctic in Question*. Toronto: Oxford University Press, 1976.

———. "Northern Sovereignty and Canadian Foreign Policy." In *The Arctic in Question*, edited by E.J. Dosman, 1-12. Toronto: Oxford University Press, 1976.

———. "The Stakes in Northern Sovereignty." In *The Arctic in Question*, edited by E.J. Dosman, 193-200. Toronto: Oxford University Press, 1976.

———. "The Northern Sovereignty Crisis, (1968-1970)." In *The Arctic in Question*, edited by E.J. Dosman, 34-57. Toronto: Oxford University Press, 1976.

Dosman E.J., and Frances Abele, "Offshore Diplomacy in the Canadian Arctic," *Journal of Canadian Studies* Vol. 16 (2) (Summer 1981).

Douglas, C.H. "Terrestrial Wildlife and Northern Development." In *Arctic Alternatives* edited by Pimlott et al., Ottawa: Canadian Arctic Resources Committee (1972).

Dunbar, Maria J. "The Arctic Setting." In *The Arctic Frontier*, edited by R. St. J. Macdonald, 3-25. Toronto: University of Toronto Press, 1966.

———. "Keynote Address." In *Marine Transportation and High Arctic Development: Policy Framework and Priorities, Symposium Proceedings*. Ottawa: Canadian Arctic Resources Committee, (1979): 3-15.

Dyson, John. *The Hot Arctic*. Boston: Little Brown and Co., 1980.

Eyre, Kenneth C. "Policeman and Post Officers: Canadian Sovereignty 1922 Style," *North/Nord* (May/June 1976): 2-5.

Florio, France. "Water Pollution and Related Principles of International Law," *Canadian Yearbook of International Law* 1979: 135-158.

Flynn, J. David. "The Development of Autonomy in the Northwest Territories," The Musk-Ox, No. 17 (1975): 22-31.

Frederick, Michel. "La délimitation du Plateau Continental entre Canada et les Etats-Unis dans la mer de Beaufort." *Canadian Yearbook of International Law* 1979: 30-96.

Freeman, Minnie Aodla. "ikumaaluminik-Living in Two Hells," In *A Century of Canada's Arctic Islands*, 1880-1980, edited by Morris Zaslow. Ottawa: Le Droit-Leclerc Printers, 1981.

Gellner, "The Military Task: Sovereignty, and Security, Surveillance and Control in the Far North," In *The Arctic in Question*, edited by E.J. Dosman, 85-101. Toronto: Oxford University Press, 1976.

Godsell, Philip H. *Red Hunters of the Snows*, Toronto: Ryerson Press, 1938.

Granatstein, J.L. "A Fit of Absence of Mind: Canada's National Interest in the North to 1968." In *The Arctic in Question*, edited by E.J. Dosman, 140-162. Toronto: Oxford University Press, 1976.

Griffths, Franklyn. "Canadian Sovereignty and Arctic International Relations." In *The Arctic in Question*, edited by E.J. Dosman, 140-162. Toronto: Oxford University Press, 1976.

Griffths, Franklyn. *A Northern Foreign Policy*, Toronto: Canadian Institute of International Affairs, 1979.

Hall, N. "The Arctic Pilot Project ¬Another Normal Wells," *Inuit Today* Vol. 9 (3).

Hamelin, L.E. *Canadian Nordicity: It's Your North, Too*. Translated by W. Barr. Montreal: Harvest House, 1978.

Hargrave, H.R. "Changing Settlement Patterns among the Mackenzie Eskimos of the Canadian North Western," In *Canada's Changing North*, edited by W. Wonders, 187-198. Toronto: McClelland and Stewart, 1971.

Head, Ivan L. "Canadian Claims to Territorial Sovereignty in the Arctic Regions, " *McGill Law Journal* Vol. 11: 218 (1963).

Horton, Desmond. "Cavalry or Police: Keeping the Peace on Two Adjacent Frontiers, 1870-1900." *Journal of Canadian Studies* Vol.12 (2): 27-37 (Spring 1977).

Hyde, International Law, Vol. 1, 2nd ed., 1945, p.348. Quoted in Margaret W. Norris "Boundary Problems Relating to the Sovereignty of the Canadian Arctic," *The Musk-Ox* No. 6: 42 (1969).

Innis, Harold A. *The Fur Trade in Canada*. 2nd ed. Toronto: University of Toronto Press (First edition in 1830, 2nd 1950).

Jenness, D. *Eskimo Administration: II. Canada, AINA Technical Paper*, No. 14: 43, 1930.

Jones, A.G.E. "Rear Admiral Sir William Edward Parry: A Different View," *The Musk-Ox* No.21: 3-10 (1978).

Lakhtine, V.L. 1928. *Prava na severnye polyarnye prostranstva* [Rights over the Arctic regions]. Moscow: Izdanie Litizdata, Narodnogo Komissariata po Inostrannym Delam.

———. 1930. Rights over the Arctic. *American Journal of International Law* 24:703 –717.

Lindley, M.F. 1926. *The acquisition and government of backward territory in international law: Being a treatise on the law and practice relating to colonial expansion*. London: Longmans, Green and Co.

Langford, J.W. "Marine Science, Technology and the Arctic: Some Questions and Guidelines for the Federal Government." In *The Arctic in Question*, edited by E.J. Dosman, 163-193. Toronto: Oxford University Press, 1976.

Lantis, M. "The Administration of Northern People: Canada and Alaska." In *The Arctic Frontier*, edited by R. St. J. Macdonald, 103. Toronto: University of Toronto Press, 1966.

Livingston, John. *Arctic Oil*, Toronto: CBC Publishing, 1981.

Lucas, George. "Regulation of Marine Operations in the Far North," *Canadian Issues* Vol. 3 (1): 175-186 (Spring 1980).

Mestral, A.L.C., and L.H.J. Legault, "Multilateral Negotiation Canada and the Law of the Sea Conference," *International Journal* Vol. 35: 47-69.

Miller, D.H. Political rights in the Arctic. *Foreign Affairs* 4(1):47– 60, 1925.

Mouton, M.W.The international regime of the polar regions. *Recueil des Cours*. 1962, III. Leyden: A.W.Sijthoff, 1963

Østreng, W. Norway in northern waters. In: Archer, C., and Scrivener, D., eds. *Northern waters*. London and Sydney: Croom Helm. 155 – 173, 1986

Newcombe, Hanna. "A proposal for a nuclear-free zone in the Arctic," Peace Research Vol. 12 (4): 175-182 (Oct. 1980).

Norris, Margaret W. "Boundary Problems Relating to the Sovereignty of the Canadian Arctic," The Musk-Ox No. 6: 32-58 (1969).

Oppenheim, L.F. *International Law, Vol. 1.*, Edited by H. Lauterpacht, 8th ed., London: Longmans, Green and Co., 1955.

Oror, Y., *Public Policymaking Re-examined*. Scranton: Chandler Publishing, 1968.

Permanent Court of International Justice, *Permanent Court of International Justice Transcriptions* (1933), Series A/B, No. 53. Quoted in Ivan L. Head. "Canadian Claims to Territorial Sovereignty in the Arctic Regions," *McGill Law Journal* Vol. 11: 216 (1963).

Pharand, D. *The Law of the Sea in the Arctic*. Ottawa: University of Ottawa Press, 1973.

———. "The Northwest Passage in International Law." *Canadian Yearbook of International Law* 1979: 99-133.

Public Archives of Canada, Colonial Office Papers, Series No. 42, Vol. 734, p.419. Quoted in Gordon W. Smith "Canada's Arctic Archipelago: 100 Years of Canadian Jurisdiction, Part I: The Transfer." *North/Nord* (Spring 1980): 11.

Rae, K.J. *The Political Economy of Northern Development*. Background Study No.36 prepared for the Science Council of Canada, Ottawa: Queens Printer, 1976.

Rohmer, Richard. *The Arctic Imperative: An Overview of the Energy Crisis*. Toronto: McClelland and Stewart, 1974.

Ross, W. Gilles. "Whaling, Inuit and the Arctic Islands," In *A Century of Canada's Arctic Islands, 1880-1980*, edited by Morris. Zaslow. Ottawa: Le Droit-Leclerc Printers, 1981.

Rowley, G.W. "International Scientific Relations in the Arctic." In *The Arctic Frontier*, edited by R. St. J. Macdonald, 278-292. Toronto: University of Toronto Press, 1966.

Science Council of Canada, *Northward Looking: A Strategy and a Science Policy for Northern Development*, Report No. 26, August 1977.

Shnitnikou, Yuri. "Soviet icebreaker reaches the North Pole." *Canadian Geographical Journal* Vol. 96 (1): 34-37, February 1978.

Smith, Gordon W. "The Transfer of Arctic Territories from Great Britain to Canada in 1880, and Some Related Matters, as Seen in Official Correspondence." *Arctic* Vol.14 (1): 53-73, March 1961.

———. "Sovereignty in the North: The Canadian Aspect of an International Problem," In *The Arctic Frontier*, edited by R. St. J. Macdonald, 195-218. Toronto: University of Toronto Press, 1966.

———. "Canada's Arctic Archipelago: 100 Years of Canadian Jurisdiction, Part I: The Transfer." *North/Nord* (Spring 1980): 10-15.

———. "Canada's Arctic Archipelago: 100 Years of Canadian Jurisdiction, Part II: Making the North Canadian." *North/Nord* (Summer 1980): 10-17.

Statutes of Great Britain, 58-59, Vict. c.34 (July 6, 1895), Quoted in Gordon W. Smith, 14. "Canada's Arctic Archipelago: 100 Years of Canadian Jurisdiction, Part I: The Transfer." *North/Nord* (Spring 1980), 14.

Stefansson, J. *The Northward Course of Empire*. New York: Harcourt, Brace and Co., 1922.

Strandford, Gerald B. "Canadian Perspectives on the Future Enforcement of the Exclusive Economic Zone," *Dalhousie Law Journal*, Vol 5: 73-120, 1979.

Sutherland, R.J. "The Strategic Significance of the Canadian Arctic." In *The Arctic Frontier*, edited by R. St. J. Macdonald, 262-65. Toronto: University of Toronto Press, 1966.

Usher, Peter J. *The Banklanders: Economy and Ecology of a Frontier Trapping Community, Volume 1- History MSRG71-1*, Dept. of Indian Affairs and Northern Development. Ottawa: Queen's Printer, 1970.

Wallace, Hugh. "Geographical Explorations to 1880." In *A Century of Canada's Arctic Islands*, edited by Morris Zaslow, 15-32. Ottawa: Le Droit-Leclero Printers, 1981.

Zaslow, Morris. *The Opening of the Canadian North, 1870-1914*. Toronto: McClelland and Stewart Ltd., 1971.

———. *Reading the Rocks*. Ottawa: Macmillan with the Dept. of Energy, Mines and Resources and Information Canada, 1975.

http://www.worldcat.org/title/reading-the-rocks-the-story-of-the-geological-survey-of-canada-1842-1972/oclc/2931347

Zariwny, A.R. "Politics, Administration and Problems of Community Development in the Northwest Territories." In *Policies of Northern Development*, edited by Nils Orvik, 86-106. Kingston: Group for International Politics, 1973.

Zariwny, A.R. "Administering the Arctic Islands 1880-1940: Policemen, Missionaries, Fur Traders," In *A Century of Canada's Arctic Islands*, edited by M. Zaslow, 61-78. Ottawa: Le Droit-Leclerc Printers, 1981.

ABOUT THE AUTHOR

David S. McRobert is an environmental lawyer based in southern Ontario. Between October 1994 and June 2010, he was In-House Counsel and Senior Policy Advisor at the Environmental Commissioner of Ontario and was involved in the establishment of the office. David has a B.Sc. in Biology from Trent University (1980) and a Master's degree in Environmental Studies (MES) from York University (1984). He graduated with an LL.B. degree from Osgoode Hall Law School (1987) and was admitted to the Ontario Bar in 1990.

Before joining the ECO, David was a senior policy advisor in the Waste Reduction Office in the Ontario Ministry of the Environment. From 1989 to 1991, he coordinated research and advocacy on waste management and global warming at Pollution Probe. He has also worked for the Workplace Health and Safety Agency in Toronto, the Ontario Round Table on Environment and Economy, the Ministry of Labour, and the Ministry of the Attorney General.

David has published numerous articles and reports on a range of environmental issues. In the past two decades, he has prepared a number of reports, articles, and conference papers on a range of environmental subjects, including public participation and government accountability for environmental decision-making. Between 1991 and 2009, he taught courses on environmental law and policy to undergraduate students in the Faculty of Environmental Studies at York University and the University of Toronto.

http://www.lacieg2s.ca/law/
http://www.lacieg2s.ca/public/law/dsm-vita.htm

ENDNOTES

1. L.F. Oppenheim, *International Law*, eighth edition, vol. 55 (London: Longmans, Green and Co.: 1955): 541.
2. Ibid.
3. Ibid., 543.
4. Gordon W. Smith, "Sovereignty in the North: The Canadian Aspect of an International Problem," *The Arctic Frontier* (Toronto: UTP, 1966), 195.
5. Margaret W. Norris, "Boundary Problems Relating to the Sovereignty of the Canadian Arctic," *The Musk-Ox,* no. 6 (1969): 32–58; 35.
6. Ibid., 36.
7. A. Cookie and C. Holland, *The Exploration of Northern Canada: 500 to 1920, A Chronology* (Toronto: Arctic History Press: 1978): 22–24.
8. John E. Caswell, "The Sponsors of Canadian Arctic Exploration: 1844–1859," *The Beaver: Magazine of the North* Outfit 300 (Winter 1969): 45–53.
9. A.G.E. Jones, "Rear Admiral Sir William Edward Parry: A Different View," *The Musk-Ox*, no. 21 (1978): 3-10.
10. Hugh Wallace, "Geographical Explorations to 1880," *A Century of Canada's Arctic Islands,* (Ottawa: Le Droit-Leclero Printers, 1981: 15–32.
11. Gordon W. Smith, "Canada's Arctic Archipelago: 100 Years of Canadian Jurisdiction, Part I: The Transfer," *North/Nord* (Spring 1980: 10–15, 11.
12. Public Archives of Canada, *Colonial Office Papers,* series no. 42, vol. 734: 419. Requoted in Smith, 11.
13. Smith, "Canada's Arctic Archipelago (I)," 11.
14. Ibid.
15. *Imperial Order in Council,* July 3, 1880. See Smith, op. cit. 11.
16. Gordon W. Smith, "The Transfer of Arctic Territories from Great Britain to Canada in 1880, and Some Related Matters, as Seen in Official Correspondence," *Arctic,* vol. 14, no. 1 (March 1961: 53–73; 58.
17. *Statutes of Great Britain,* 58–59, Vict. c. 34 (July 6, 1895. Requoted in Smith, 14.
18. Chamberlain to Officer Administering the Government (July 26, 1895). Requoted in Smith, 14.
19. Smith, "Canada's Arctic Archipelago (I)," 14.
20. Ibid., 15.

21. Ibid.
22. F.J. Alcock, "Albert Peter Low," *The Canadian Geographical Journal,* vol. 38, no.4 (April 1954: 160–163.
23. Gordon W. Smith, "Canada's Arctic Archipelago: 100 Years of Canadian Jurisdiction, Part II: Making the North Canadian," *North/Nord* (Summer 1980: 10-17; 4.
24. Kenneth C. Eyre, "Policeman and Post Officers: Canadian Sovereignty 1922 Style," *North/Nord* (May/June 1976): 2-5; 5.
25. Smith, "Canada's Arctic Archipelago (II)," 10.
26. Ibid., 5.
27. Smith, "Canadian Arctic Archipelago (II)," 15.
28. Smith, "Canada's Arctic Archipelago (II)," 15.
29. Morris Zaslow, "Administering the Arctic Islands 1880-1940: Policemen, Missionaries, Fur Traders," *A Century of Canada's Arctic Islands* (Ottawa: Le Droit-Leclerc Printers, 1981): 61–78.
30. Smith, "Canada's Arctic Archipelago (II)," 14.
31. Zaslow, "Administering the Arctic Islands," 63.
32. Smith, "Canada's Arctic Archipelago (II)," 15.
33. Eyre, "Policemen and Post Offices," 3.
34. Cited in Smith, "Canada's Arctic Archipelago (II)," 14.
35. Smith, "Canada's Arctic Archipelago (II)," 14.
36. Lanslow, "Administering the Arctic Islands," 67.
37. Smith suggests that there may have been other reasons for canceling the expedition, including the poor weather, late season, and numerous accidents. Apparently Macmillan had already asked Washington by wireless for permission to end the expedition before their encounter with the *Arctic.* However, it is unclear to what degree this meeting influenced further activity by the U.S. in the Archipelago.
38. H.A. Innis, *The Fur Trade in Canada* (Toronto: UTP, first edition in 1830, second 1950): 280.
39. Innis, 286–287.
40. K.J. Rae, *The Political Economy of Northern Development*, background study no. 36 for the Science Council of Canada (Ottawa: Queens Printer, 1976): 38-39. Innis also elaborates extensively on early transportation in *The Fur Trade in Canada,* 345–354.
41. Morris Zaslow, *The Opening of the Canadian North 1870-1914,* (Toronto: McClelland and Stewart Ltd., 1971).
42. Innis, *The Fur Trade,* 343–354.
43. Peter J. Usher, *The Banklanders: Economy and Ecology of a Frontier Trapping Community,* vol. 1, History MSRG71-1, Dept. of Indian Affairs and Northern Development (Ottawa: Queen's Printer, 1970).
44. Ibid., 45.

45. Ibid., 51.
46. Ibid., 54.
47. W. Gillies Ross, "Whaling, Inuit, and the Arctic Islands," *A Century of Canada's Arctic Islands, 1880-1980.*
48. Philip H. Godsell, *Red Hunters of the Snows* (Toronto: Ryerson Press, 1938): 272. Godsell gives an account of thirty years' experience with the primitive Indians and Inuit tribes of the Canadian northwest and Arctic coast, with a brief history of the early contact between white fur traders and the native peoples.
49. D. Jenness, *Eskimo Administration: II.* Canada, AINA Technical Paper, no. 14, 43.
50. Laslow, *The Opening of the Canadian North,* 256–258.
51. H.R. Hargrave, "Changing Settlement Patterns among the Mackenzie Eskimos of the Canadian North Western," *Canada's Changing North* (Toronto: McClelland and Stewart, 1971): 187–198.
52. Zaslow, *The Opening of the Canadian North,* 270.
53. W. Gillies Ross, 48–50.
54. Godsell, *Red Hunter,* 270–274.
55. Zaslow, *The Opening of the Canadian North,* 270.
56. Ibid.
57. Godsell, *Red Hunter,* 276–277.
58. Jenness, *Eskimo Administration.*
59. Zaslow, *The Opening of the Canadian North,* 101–123.
60. Rae, *The Political Economy of Northern Development,* 60.
61. Ibid., 61–64.
62. Ibid., 70-74
63. Jenness, *Eskimo Administration,* 23–24.
64. Zaslow, *The Opening of the Canadian North,* 127.
65. Ibid., 224–226.
66. Ibid., 228–231.
67. P. Cummings and N.Y. Mickenburg, *Native Rights in Canada* (Toronto: General Publishing, 1972): 128.
68. M. Lantis, "The Administration of Northern People: Canada and Alaska," *The Arctic Frontier,* 103.
69. Ibid., 104.
70. Michael Dear, "Planning Community Health Services in Arctic Canada," *The Musk-Ox,* no. 19 (1976): 28–36.
71. Charles S. Brant and Charels W. Hobart, "Eskimo Education, Danish and Canadian: A Comparison," *The Canadian Review of Sociology and Anthropology,* vol. 2 (May 1966): 47–66; 48.
72. Ibid., 53.

73. A.R. Zariwny, "Politics, Administration and Problems of Community Development in the Northwest Territories," *Policies of Northern Development* (Kingston: Group for International Politics, 1973): 86–106.

74. Hugh Brody, *The Peoples Land* (Markham, Ont.: Penguin, 1975) and Minnie Aodla Freeman, "ikumaaluminik-Living in Two Hells," *A Century of Canada's Arctic Islands.*

75. Jenness, *Eskimo Administration.*

76. Ibid.

77. L.E. Hamelin, *Canadian Nordicity: It's Your North, Too* (Montreal: Harvest House, 1978)

78. Brody, *The Peoples Land.*

79. J. David Flynn, "The Development of Autonomy in the Northwest Territories, *The Musk-Ox,* no. 17 (1975): 22–31, 24.

80. Ibid., 26.

81. While Hamelin has pointed out that more than one-quarter of the seventy-eight communities have no form of government at all. Many of these communities are DEW Line sites. While it might be desirable for these communities to have some say over their affairs, it probably isn't that realistic. Most DEW Line sites have fewer than twenty men and their personnel is rotated every six months. As Flynn suggests, these settlements, like company towns in the mid-North, resemble office buildings or factories more than developing communities.

82. R.J Sutherland, "The Strategic Significance of the Canadian Arctic," *The Arctic Frontier,* 262–265.

83. T.E Armstrong, "The Strategic Significance of the Canadian Arctic," *The Arctic Frontier,* 262–265.

84. Sutherland, "Strategic Significance," 273.

85. Zaslow provides many vivid descriptions of these activities in *The Opening of the Canadian North.*

86. Desmond Horton, "Cavalry or Police: Keeping the Peace on Two Adjacent Frontiers, 1870-1900," *Journal of Canadian Studies,* vol. 12 no. 2 (Spring 1977): 27–37; 34.

87. Zaslow, *The Circumpolar North,* 118.

88. Armstrong, *The Circumpolar North,* 118.

89. Department of Indian Affairs and Northern Development, *Canada's North Today,* (Ottawa: Supplies and Services, 1978)): 28–29.

90. Morris Zaslow, *Reading the Rocks* (Ottawa: Macmillan with the Dept. of Energy, Mines and Resources and Information Canada, 1975)

91. Ibid., 290.

92. Ibid., 264.

93. Ibid., 266.

94. Ibid., 269–275.

95. Ibid., 273.

96. Ibid., 311.

97. Ibid., 346.

98. Rae, *The Political Economy of Northern Development,* 108.

99. C.H. Douglas, "Terrestrial Wildlife and Northern Development," *Arctic Alternatives* (Ottawa: CARC, 1972): 194–234.

100. E.J. Dosman, ed., *The Arctic in Question* (Toronto: Oxford U. Press, 1976) and Richard Rohmer, *The Arctic Imperative* (Toronto: McClelland and Stewart, 1974).

101. Dosman, "Northern Sovereignty and Canadian Foreign Policy," *The Arctic in Question,* 1–12.

102. J.L. Granatstein, "A Fit of Absence of Mind: Canada's National Interest in the North to 1968," *The Arctic in Question,* 140–162.

103. F. Griffths, "Canadian Sovereignty and Arctic International Relations," *The Arctic in Question,* 140–162.

104. Dosman, "The Stakes in Northern Sovereignty," *The Arctic in Question,* 193–200; 195–196.

105. R.B. Bryers, "Sovereignty and Canadian Foreign Policy: The Need for Enforcement Capability," *The Arctic in Question,* 58–84, 76.

106. J.W. Langford, "Marine Science, Technology and the Arctic: Some Questions and Guidelines for the Federal Government," *The Arctic in Question,* 163–193, 170.

107. Gellner, "The Military Task: Sovereignty, and Security, Surveillance and Control in the Far North," *The Arctic in Question,* 85–101, 90.

108. Ibid., 99.

109. Rohmer, *The Arctic Imperative.*

110. Dyson, *The Hot Arctic,* 179–185.

111. Byers, 90.

112. Byers, 91.

113. Department of Defence, *Foreign Policy for Canadians* (Ottawa: Queens Printer, 1970).

114. *Debates,* 1906-1907, Senate, Canada, 271, op. cit., by M. Morris, "Boundary Problems," 54.

115. M. Morris, "Boundary Problems," 53.

116. Ivan L. Head, "Canadian Claims to Territorial Sovereignty in the Arctic Regions, " *McGill Law Journal* vol. 11 (1963), 218.

117. Hyde, *International Law,* vol. 1 (second ed., 1945), 348. See Morris, "Boundary Problems," op. cit., 42.

118. Smith, "Sovereignty in the North," 214–218.

119. Head, 205.

120. Morris, 329.

121. Ibid.

122. D. Pharand, *The Law of the Sea in the Arctic* (Ottawa: University of Ottawa Press, 1973).

123. J.E. Bernier, Report on the Dominion Government Expedition to the Arctic Islands, etc., 1906-07 (Ottawa: Kings Printer, 1910), 192–195. Cited from Zaslow, *The Opening of the Canadian North,* 267.

124. "The Clipperton Island Award, 26 Jan. 1931," *American Journal of International Law* 390 (1932): 393-4.

125. Michel Frederick, "La de limitation du Plateau Continental entre Le Canada et les Etats-Uria dans la mer de Beaufort," *Canadian Yearbook of International Law 1979*, 30–96.

126. E.J. Dosman and Frances Abele, "Offshore Diplomacy in the Canadian Arctic," *Journal of Canadian Studies* vol. 16, no. 2 (Summer 1981): 7.

127. (1974) Canada Treaty Series No. 9.

128. Dosman and Abele, "Offshore Diplomacy," 9.

129. Permanent Court of International Justice, Transcriptions (1933), Series A/B, no. 53. Cited in Head, "Canadian Claims," 216.

130. Ibid.

131. "The Clipperton Island Award," *A.J.I.L.* See note 124.

132. Dobel, "The Policy Dimension," *The Arctic in Question,* 121–139, 136.

133. Ibid.

134. Pharand, *The Law of the Sea in the Arctic.*

135. Dosman, "The Northern Sovereignty Crisis (1968-1970)," *The Arctic in Question,* 34-57; 39. 136. W. Clemens, "Ecology and International Relations," *International Journal*, vol. 28 (Winter 1972–1973), 1–28.

137. Dosman, "The Northern Sovereignty Crisis."

138. Balaram B. Dey, Shipping routes, ice cover and year-round navigation in the Canadian Arctic, *Polar Record* Vol. 20 (129): 549-559, 1981. As Dey explained, past forecasts by geologists of potentially large oil and natural gas reserves in the North American Arctic (e.g., Prudhoe Bay, the Mackenzie delta, and the Canadian Arctic islands) are coming closer to reality. Results from Canmar (Canadian Marine Drilling Ltd of Calgary) drill ships working in the southern Beaufort Sea continue to support the prediction of considerable hydrocarbon deposits in this area. The most significant discovery, gas amounting to 0.48–0.50 trillion m3 [17–18 trillion ft3] was made by Panarctic Oils Limited in the Canadian High Arctic in the late 1970s, in particular the Drake field off Melville Island and the surrounding region. In the early 1980s Panarctic Oils was a government-industry consortium; Petro-Canada owned 45 per cent of the shares and provides the bulk of the exploration budget.

139. D. Pharand, "The Northwest Passage in International Law," *Canadian Yearbook of International Law 1979,* 99–133; 132–133.

140. Evan Browns, "Sovereignty Questions Remain after Century in the Arctic," *International Perspectives,* (July/August 1980): 7–11.

141. Ibid., 10.

142. A.L.C. Mestral and L.H.J. Legault, "Multilateral Negotiation Canada and the Law of the Sea Conference, " *International Journal* vol. 35, 47–69.

143. Ibid., 69.

144. Stefansson, *The Northward Course of Empire* (New York: Harcourt, Brace and Co., 1922), 1.

145. Ibid., 10.

146. Yuri Shnitnikou, "Soviet Icebreaker Reaches the North Pole." *Canadian Geographical Journal* vol. 96 no.1 (February 1978): 34–37.

147. Maria Dunbar, "The Arctic Setting," *The Arctic Frontier*, 3–25.

148. Franklyn Griffths, *A Northern Foreign Policy* (Toronto: Canadian Institute of International Affairs, 1979): 16.

149. G.W. Rowley, "International Scientific Relations in the Arctic" *The Arctic Frontier*, 278–292.

150. Armstrong et al., *The Circumpolar North*, 268.

151. Ibid,. 246

152. Science Council of Canada, *Northward Looking: A Strategy and a Science Policy for Northern Development*, Report no. 26 (August 1977).

153. Armstrong et al., *The Circumpolar North*, 269.

154. Griffths, *A Northern Foreign Policy*, 43–48

155. Hanna Newcombe, "A Proposal for a Nuclear-free Zone in the Arctic," Peace Research vol. 12, no.4 (October 1980): 175–182.

156. Gerald B. Strandford, "Canadian Perspectives on the Future Enforcement of the Exclusive Economic Zone," *Dalhousie Law Journal*, vol. 5 (1979): 73–120.

157. Armstrong et al., *The Circumpolar North*, 253.

158. M.J. Dunbar, "Keynote Address," *Marine Transportation and High Arctic Development: Policy Framework and Priorities, Symposium Proceedings* (Ottawa: CARC, 1979): 3–15.

159. John Livingston, *Arctic Oil* (Toronto: CBC Publishing, 1981).

160. France Florio, "Water Pollution and Related Principles of International Law," *Canadian Yearbook of International Law 1979*, 135–158.

161. Ibid.

162. Ibid., see also Griffths, *A Northern Foreign Policy.*

163. John Dyson, *The Hot Arctic* (Boston: Little Brown and Co., 1980).

164. Griffths, *A Northern Foreign Policy*, 17.

165. George Lucas, "Regulation of Marine Operations in the Far North," *Canadian Issues* vol. 3, no.1 (Spring 1980): 175–186.

166. Dosman and Abele, "Offshore Diplomacy," 14.

167. Y. Oror, Public Policymaking Re-examined (Scranton: Chandler Publishing, 1968).

168. Ibid., 160.

169. N. Hall, "The Arctic Pilot Project- Another Normal Wells," *Inuit Today*, vol. 9 no.3, 8–12; 43.

H. Jenkyn's Memo on the proposed Colonial Boundaries Act.
(cited from Interior Dept., Dom. Lands Branch Correspondence
1895, File No. 284096(Public Archives of Canada) R.G. 15,
B-1a(220), Memo by H. Jenkyns(May 21, 1895). Quoted by
Smith, "Canada's Arctic Archipelago: II", p.14.)

It appears from three reports from the Law Officers, dated respectively the 25th August 1894, the 27th February 1895, and the 27th February 1895 [sic], that the law as to the alteration of the boundaries of colonies is as follows: —

I. Where an Imperial Act has expressly defined the boundaries of a colony or has bestowed a constitution on a colony within certain boundaries, territory cannot be annexed to that Colony so as to be completely fused with it, as e.g., by being included in a province or electoral division of it, without statutory authority . . .

II. But the Queen can, unless restrained by an Imperial Act, give to any such colony as above mentioned and the colony can accept the administration and government of any territory. The most solemn mode of such acceptance is colonial legislation.

In such a cse [sic] the territory is not incorporated with and does not become part of the colony, but is only administered by the same government.

III. The same law appears to apply — (a) Where the boundaries have been fixed by Order in Council or letters patent issued in pursuance of statutory authority . . . .

V. An annexation, even if irregular in the outset, may possibly, if followed by a de facto incorporation for a long period of time, acquire, like any other constitutional changes, validity through usage . . . .

It follows from the above that certain annexations of territory by Order in Council and letters patent accompanied by Acts of the Colonial Legislatures are invalid. For instance —

(a) The annexation to Canada of all British territory in North America and of the adjacent islands by Order in Council of the 31st July 1880 (the limits of the Dominion having been fixed by the British North America Acts, 1867 and 1871).
(b) The annexation to Queensland of all islands within 60 miles of the coast of Queensland . . .
(c) The annexation to New Zealand of the Kermadec Islands . . .

It will be observed that the Bill applies only where the boundary has been fixed by or under an Act of Parliament, and does not touch the case where the boundaries have been already fixed by the prerogative power of the Queen 5